HOW TO PRAY & COMMUNICATE WITH GOD

by Dr. Walter L. Banks

Edited with Case Study Applications
by Dr. Colleen Birchett

umi

urban ministries, inc.
1439 W. 103rd Street
Chicago, IL 60643

Publisher
Urban Ministries, Inc.
1439 W. 103rd St.
Chicago, Illinois 60643
(312) 233-4499

ISBN: 940955-06-7
Catalog No. 9-2732

Scripture quotations are from the *King James Version* of the Bible.

Printed in the United States of America

Dedicated to the memory of
Dr. Walter L. Banks
and to his wife,
Mrs. Irene Banks

Contents

Foreword

> Steal away, Steal away, Steal away to Jesus! Steal away, Steal away home, ain't got long to stay here.
>
> My Lord, He calls me, He calls me by the thunder; The trumpet sounds within my soul; I ain't got long to stay here.
>
> Green trees are bending; Poor sinners stand a trembling; The trumpet sounds within my soul; I ain't got long to stay here!
>
> My Lord, he calls me, He calls me by the lightning; The trumpet sounds within my soul; I ain't got long to stay here!
>
> Steal away, Steal away, Steal away to Jesus! Steal away, Steal away home! I ain't got long to be here.[1]

No one really knows when, where or who composed the song *"Steal Away."* It is one of the many melodies that sprang forth from the breasts of Black slaves as, collectively and individually, they drew near to God. It is just one of many descriptions of corporate and individual prayer which took place at a time when it was illegal for Black people to "hold church" in America.

No doubt it was composed during the wee hours of the morning while white police officers napped after patrolling the Black community all night to prevent Black people from worshiping God together. If you were standing near any southern creek, in the wee hours of the morning, you might hear this and other songs as a small

Black prayer band of believers emerged from the swamps to "steal away" to Jesus. For many slaves, these small prayer meetings were the happiest times of their lives.

Indeed, stealing away to Jesus became a tradition among Black Americans. Out of this tradition came many other melodies celebrating the joys of communicating with God.

> Now let us...Have a little talk with Jesus. Let us...tell Him all about our troubles. He will...Hear our faintest cry and He will...answer by and by. Now when you...feel a little prayer wheel turning, and you...know a little fire is burning You will...find a little talk with Jesus makes it right. It makes it right![2]

Prayer is the subject of this first of a series of books based on the broadcasts of Dr. Walter Banks over Moody Bible Institute Radio. Dr. Banks produced the series entitled, "Let Us Pray," during the years prior to his going home to be with the Lord in June of 1986.

> "We live with the consciousness that we are not sufficient in ourselves...we don't have the knowledge that we need to have; therefore we seek the aid of Him who is our Lord."

These words are among the many reflections of Dr. Banks, and they represent one of the basic themes of the book. Dr. Banks recognized both the power and the necessity of personal communication with God.

In this short book, Dr. Banks' messages on prayer are presented in print form. They comprise twelve chapters. Each chapter is accompanied by a "Case Study in Prayer" developed by Dr. Colleen Birchett, editor of the series. Each case study guides the reader into an in-depth study of a prayer from the Bible. The prayers that have been selected are ones which exemplify the principles Dr.

Banks teaches within the chapter

Objectives of the Book. Upon completion of this book, the reader should be able to use the principles taught by Dr. Banks (and gleaned from the study of the sample prayers) to better pray and communicate with God. The book is designed so that it can also be used in group study, and in church training sessions.

The Content. Chapters 1-8 provide principles for improving personal communications with God. Chapters 9-11 contain guidelines for intercessory prayer. Chapter 12 provides guidelines for private, corporate (public) and professional prayer. The book also includes a bibliography of books about prayer. Many of the books contained in the bibliography are by Black authors.

The Organization of the Book. With the exception of the introduction, each chapter is divided into two parts. Part One contains the edited transcripts of Dr. Banks' radio broadcasts, along with the Scriptures to which he refers.

Part Two of each chapter contains a "Case Study in Prayer." A prayer from the Bible is presented, along with a series of exercises designed to lead the reader into an in-depth study of the prayer and an application of points made by Dr. Banks in the chapter. Each case study contains three types of exercises: "discovery" exercises, "summary exercises" and "applications."

Uses. This book can be used for private as well as group study. It can be used as a Sunday School elective. It can be used during training hour, to train all church workers and "bench members." It can also be used during weekday Bible studies as a Bible study guide, and it can be used in family devotions. In fact, it may be used as a foundation for a church-wide retreat.

Private Study. If used as a private devotional guide, it might be useful to spread the material out over weeks or perhaps months. Select a different chapter each week or month. Then select different exercises each day until the exercises for a given chapter are exhausted.

Once the chapters on prayer are completed, it might be useful to begin reading some of the books and articles listed in the bibliography, while continuing to practice the presence of God through prayer.

Group Study—90 Minute Sessions. The book is designed for a two-part group study session. Part I would be a time when participants, under the direction of a group leader (or minister), study the transcript of Dr. Banks' tape and the Scriptures to which he refers. This initial study session would require about 30 minutes. Then the group leader would begin the "laboratory" session. In the laboratory session, the group would, collectively, investigate a model prayer from the Bible.

The group study session is designed so that every person can contribute something to the understanding and application of the model prayer. This process would begin as the group leader divides the larger group into smaller groups. The number of smaller groups would vary according to the number of "discovery" exercises contained in a given chapter. Each small group would be assigned a separate exercise from the set available.

A small group leader would be appointed (or elected) for each small group. Within the small groups, the small group leader would assign one (or two, depending on the size of the group) questions to each participant. In the event that there are more participants in a small group than there are questions, then people might work on questions in two's, three's (or more).

About ten minutes should be allowed for each small group participant to answer the questions related to each exercise. Then another ten minutes should be allowed for participants to present their answers to the questions to the small group of which they are a part. The remainder of the time should be spent allowing the small group to discuss the "summary question," the last question of each exercise.

At the end of the small group discussions, the smaller groups would convene with the larger group again. In the larger group, a spokesperson from each group would summarize their small group discussion. Then the larger group, under the direction of the original leader, would discuss the final "Summary Exercise" and the "Application" at the end of the chapter's "Case Study in Prayer."

Group Study—60 Minute Sessions. In shorter periods, it might be necessary to use part of a given chapter as a stimulus for discussion during the group meeting itself. Then the other part of the chapter might be used as a "homework" assignment or for private devotional study.

Family Devotions. During the week preceding the study of a given chapter, all members would read a given chapter privately, along with the prayer "Case Study" at the end of the chapter. Each member would select a different related "discovery" exercise and, on the basis of it, prepare a short presentation for family devotions.

The devotional period would begin with a discussion of the points Dr. Banks makes in the chapter. Then the model prayer from the case study would be read. Each member would present insights he/she has, based on the exercise (related to the model prayer) that was completed during the week. After each member has contributed, then the family would discuss the "Summary Exercise" and "Application" at the end of each chapter case study.

In summary, the book can be used in many ways. However, the main purpose is the one that was articulated by Dr. Banks so many times over his radio broadcasts—that Christians everywhere would learn to "pray without ceasing," and to commune with God regularly.

1. American Negro Melody, "Steal Away to Jesus,"

The New National Baptist Hymnal (Nashville: National Baptist Publishing Board, 1977), p. 477.

2. Cleavant Derricks, "Just a Little Talk with Jesus," *The New National Baptist Hymnal* (Nashville: National Baptist Publishing Board, 1977), p. 298.

Acknowledgments

We wish to acknowledge several persons without whose help this manuscript would not have come into being. First and foremost, of course, we thank the late Dr. Walter Banks who worked tirelessly to develop the content for the radio broadcast series, "Let Us Pray," and delivered the series over Moody Bible Institute Radio. Next, we wish to thank Perry C. Straw of Moody Bible Institute who donated the radio tapes of Dr. Walter Banks to Urban Outreach, and who permitted us to present the tapes in the current print format.

We also wish to thank Mrs. Irene Banks, wife of Dr. Banks for allowing us to use the tapes as we saw fit.

We also wish to acknowledge the contributions of Mrs. Sara Hennings who so graciously transcribed the tapes so that we could edit them for preparation for print. Then of course, we wish to acknowledge the contributions of Publications Manager, Shawan Brand and Mary Lewis, Copy Editor. Last but not least, of course, we wish to thank Grant Hoeskstra and his staff for graphics and layout.

Introduction

The phrase "let us pray" is a very common word of exhortation. In church and in other groups we often say, "let us pray" at some point in the discussion. Oh, how much we lack an understanding of what we are really saying.

Prayer as Communication. Prayer has to do with communication. We have been created as rational beings, and this implies that we have a capacity both to send and to receive communication. That is, we can and do receive communication from our Lord and we can and will respond to His communication.

A good idea of communication is that of the radio and the sending station. The transmitting station sends out signals. If there were no receiving set, there would be no point in sending the signals. God is a personal being, which involves His being a rational being. He has set out through His Word and through His messengers, communication to us. That is recorded in His Word. Were it not possible for us to receive and respond to that communication, He would not have sent it.

Correspondingly, those to whom the signal is sent not only have the opportunity, privilege and mechanics for receiving it, but they can also respond to Him. Prayer is then a real and definite sense of communication with God.

Expressions of Prayer. There are a variety of expressions used as we think of the word "prayer." We do not have the space to exhaust all that the Bible says on this subject. However, there are any number of expressions that we might use to conceptualize prayer. From the Old Testament word itself, prayer means to entreat, to implore, to intercede, to utter, to ask, to make a request and to beseech. These are some of the ideas of the original Hebrew use of the word.

It is interesting that the first time we see the word in its Old Testament form, it is in the Book of Genesis and relates to Abraham. In Genesis 20, we find that Abraham had a very unfortunate experience. He had the need to gather food. A famine was in the land. Abraham had journeyed toward the South country and was dwelling between Kaddesh and Shur in Gerar. Here, he said that his wife was his sister. He got himself into problems because the men among whom he came to dwell took his wife unto themselves.

It was in relationship to Abraham's problem that God told Abimelech (20:7) to restore Abraham to his wife, for Abraham was a prophet and Abraham would pray for Abimelech. The verse says "He will pray for you."

In Genesis 4:26, the expression "call upon the name of the Lord" is introduced. This use of the term prayer was following the experience of Cain and Abel when Cain slew his brother and when God later gave Eve another son. Eve said that she had been given this son of the Lord. At that point, the Bible says that "men began to call on the name of the Lord."

Therefore "Calling upon God" is one of the titles or one of the descriptive phrases for prayer. This idea of calling upon God is expressed throughout the Bible. In fact, a refusal to call upon God indicates that a person is not in the right relationship with God, or he is not knowledgeable of God. Refusing to call upon God indicates that the person so doing is ignorant of God.

Praying People in the Bible. There are so many illustrations of people praying in the Bible. Daniel readily comes to mind. Daniel prayed three times each day. Then there is David. David also prayed several times each day. David speaks of praying in the morning, at noon, in the evening and throughout the night. David had the confident assurance that he would be heard by God. Both David and Daniel were strong men of prayer.

Then there is Hezekiah, one of the good kings of the Old Testament. Hezekiah was a man who really was "pressed out of measure" in many areas of his life. First of all, because there was so much widespread evil, he had to seek the guidance of the Lord in order to remove some of it. Hezekiah also had the need for military and armies to fight off those who were pressing against him. Due to the threats made by superior forces, Hezekiah became a man of prayer.

In the New Testament, we find other examples of people of prayer. In the New Testament, there is no greater example than our Lord Jesus Christ. The Gospel of Luke shows, without a shadow of a doubt, what prayer meant to our Lord Jesus Christ. Jesus prayed without ceasing. He is seen praying in the morning, a great while before day. If Jesus had the necessity to pray, certainly we do.

The Aims of This Study on Prayer. Throughout this study on prayer, we will be underscoring the fact that the heart needs to be attuned to the needs of those around us. We will be pointing out the many organized lists of things for which we ought to pray. The Apostle Paul gives us these and we will deal with many of them as we examine some of the many models of prayer in the Bible.

We will also underscore that it is important to prepare for prayer. If we prepare our Sunday School lessons, if we prepare our sermons and if we prepare for other kinds of encounters, we should also be willing to prepare to pray. We prepare so that the content of our prayers will be according to the discretion of the Holy Spirit.

As we study prayer, we must keep in mind that

prayer is necessary because God commanded it. The commands are set forth in both the Old and New Testaments. We must also keep in mind that Christ guaranteed results from prayer. In many biblical passages, Christ tells us what will happen as a result of right praying.

I trust that the Lord my God will use this study on prayer to guide our hearts into examining those areas where we need to be a little more solicitous of God, and a little more diligent in our spiritual lives. May God guide us and direct us as we embark upon this study of prayer.

CHAPTER ONE

Praying Without Ceasing

We begin our study of prayer with an examination of the concept of praying without ceasing.

from Scripture
Luke 18:1 *And He spake a parable unto them to this*
end, that men ought always to pray, and not to faint;
2 *Saying, There was in a city a judge, which feared*
not God, neither regarded man:
3 *And there was a widow in that city; and she came*
unto him, saying, Avenge me of mine adversary.
4 *And he would not for a while: but afterward he said*
within himself, Though I fear not God, nor regard man;
5 *Yet because this widow troubleth me, I will avenge*
her, lest by her continual coming she weary me.
6 *And the Lord said, Hear what the unjust judge*
saith.
7 *And shall not God avenge his own elect, which cry*
day and night unto him, though he bear long with them?
8 *I tell you that he will avenge them speedily....*
Colossians 1:3 *We give thanks to God and the Father of*
our Lord Jesus Christ, praying always for you,
4 *Since we heard of your faith in Christ Jesus, and of*
the love which ye have to all the saints,
5 *For the hope which is laid up for you in heaven,*
whereof ye heard before in the word of truth of the gospel;
3:1 If ye then be risen with Christ, seek those things
which are above, where Christ sitteth on the right hand
of God.
2 *Set your affection on things above, not on things on*
the earth.
1 Thessalonians 5:17 *Pray without ceasing.*

Scripture Discussion

Exactly what is meant by the expression, "pray without ceasing"? In the above Scriptures, our Lord has said men are always to pray, and Paul says pray without ceasing. Are we to understand that this matter of prayer is to be something that we're to be occupied with all of the time? I can't conceive that this is really the meaning of these two expressions. Therefore, let us "tear apart" some of what may be involved in praying without ceasing and come to grips with it in a more realistic way.

Walking in the Spirit. First of all, we can be sure that the Lord Jesus would not want us to pray all of the time. There are other things that God has put on our list of items to do. For example, we must bear testimony to Him. We must grow in grace, and we are to respond in other ways to that which He has given us in His Word. Of course, the Apostle Paul, who says we should pray without ceasing, has prayer on a list of a number of other things that are involved in the Christian life.

So in form, we cannot always be praying. That is, there must be a difference between the instance of prayer and the form of prayer as we normally think of it. As to the form of prayer itself, it is not intended that we should always be on our knees, or that we should always be uttering statements or making requests of God. Instead, praying without ceasing has to do with our inner condition—our spiritual life. It has to do with walking in the Spirit.

We're told in several portions of the Word, particularly in Galatians 5:16, that we ought to "Walk in the Spirit." We are told that if we "walk in the Spirit" we will not fulfill the laws of the flesh.

This suggests that, to pray without ceasing, we must

be so taken up with what it means to be in Christ, with what it means to be a member of the family of God, and with what it means to be a servant of Christ that we are occupied with the Spirit of God in all respects: attitude, words and actions. In so doing, we can, at any time, and at all times, relate to Him in communion.

Although we might not always be saying things, we may always be making expressions to Him in a form of communication. The readiness of our hearts and minds that would result certainly suggests what is meant by "pray without ceasing."

This means that we would set our affections on heavenly things, not on matters of this earth (Colossians 3:1-2). If we set our affections and the bent of our minds on Christ, then we would have no difficulty in praying without ceasing or always being in prayer. A prayerful attitude of heart, and a prayerful attitude of mind is what is involved.

Following the Example of Our Lord Jesus Christ. There are other examples in Scripture of praying without ceasing. The Lord Jesus Christ provides one example. Our Lord is seen conducting a very serious ministry of teaching. The Lord Jesus had a very rigorous teaching routine and much of it had to do with rejecting the statements and attitudes of men.

He is seen exhorting and upbraiding the cities, pronouncing woe upon them, and telling them that it would be more tolerable for certain cities of the Old Testament in the day of judgment than for the cities in which He was preaching that day (Matthew 11:20-22).

However, immediately within this same context, we find that the Lord entered into communion with His Father. Jesus found the time to say,

> I thank thee, O Father, Lord of heaven and earth, because thou hast hid these things from the wise and prudent, and hast

> revealed them unto babes. Even so, Father: for so it seemed good in thy sight. All things are delivered unto me of my Father: and no man knoweth the Son, but the Father; neither knoweth any man the Father, save the Son, and he to whomsoever the Son will reveal him. (Matthew 11:25-27)

This is a good illustration of what it means to be "instant in prayer" (Romans 12:12) or to be praying always (1 Thessalonians 5:17). The Lord Jesus knew that His ministry was being fulfilled in the light of a commission that God had given Him. However, the Lord remained in a prayerful attitude.

As a result of this, the Lord Jesus did not have to repent for anything that He was not doing or for omitting something that He should have been doing. He did not have to sit down and clear His heart and mind of any of the dirt that might have been in a mortal heart. It would have hindered God from hearing Him. He knew that constantly, daily, He was living in the light of the will of God. As a result of that, He could turn from one aspect of His ministry to another.

Therefore, He intends that we, by living in the Spirit, and by walking according to the dictates of the Spirit of God, through the word of God, be able (whether it is a matter of some "spiritual exercise" or another occasion) to be so filled with knowledge and committed to Him, that we will be ready at all times to pray.

Our Lord's example also suggests that we must live with the consciousness of knowing that we're not sufficient in ourselves, either for the wisdom that we need or for the strength that we must have. We don't have the knowledge that we need to have. We are always ready to seek the aid and the instruction of Him who is our Lord. This, of course, provides us with a readiness in prayer. The Lord Jesus exemplified it for us.

Following the Apostle Paul's Example. The Apostle Paul provides yet another example. In his writing to the Colossian Christians, he indicates he realizes that God has done a great work in their midst. In Colossians 1:3, he says to the Colossian Christians, "We give thanks to God and the Father of our Lord Jesus Christ, praying always for you." Although Paul says here that he prays always, it is certain that he had to engage in other labors.

However, in mentioning the Colossian Christians, he says that they were always in his heart, that they were always on his mind and that he was therefore in a constant state of being aware of their needs. He said,

> Since we heard of your faith in Christ Jesus, and of the love which ye have to all the saints, for the hope that is laid up for you in heaven, whereof ye heard before in the word of the truth of the gospel...For this cause we also, since the day we heard it, do not cease to pray for you... (1:4-5, 9)

Paul's method of praying is unknown.

However, throughout the history of the church there have been men who have spent long hours in prayer. We are told that men such as John Wesley and some of the Protestant Reformers spent two and three hours each day in prayer. This may also have been true of Paul.

However, he says to the Colossian Christians, "I do not cease to pray for you."

In his not ceasing to pray for them, he had in mind the resources that they needed and that they did not have these resources in themselves alone. Paul had learned what the Lord Jesus Christ said:

> I am the vine, ye are the branches: He that abideth in me, and I in him, the same bringeth forth much fruit: for without me ye can do nothing. (John 15:5)

Paul realized that in order for them to develop as he knew God would develop them through their own energies, they must be in a constant attitude of submission to Him. Using himself as an example, he was really saying, "I have prayed and am praying always for you."

In relationship to our ministries, we realize that we are not sufficient. It is evident that the Apostle Paul came to that realization also. He realized that prayer for those to whom the Lord had led him was vital. Regarding this need for prayer, then, he said that he did not cease to pray for them.

Praying for Others without Ceasing. Many of us have had the experience of having the Lord bring to our minds people with whom we have been associated in some way or another. He brings them to our minds at times when there is a special need in their lives. We have also heard of instances where a person's mind, in the middle of the night or at some other time went to a given person or to that person's circumstances. Suddenly that person was led to pray for the other person. Later, it was found that the person prayed for had an urgent need and that the Spirit of God had prompted the believer to lay hold on Him for that person for a very specific purpose.

This situation is another example of what Paul had in mind when he said, "I cease not to pray for you." One notices an openness on his part that was unhindered. The fellowship between him and the Holy Spirit was such that the Spirit could at any moment bring to his mind those for whom he needed to make a request. Certainly his heart was always open, for their good and for their blessing. Paul realized that not only in his own relationship to others was there a need for this "constancy" in prayer, but he also encouraged others to pray for him.

Pointing out the need for prayer, Paul emphasized the need to pray always with supplication and thanksgiving. He says, in Ephesians 5:19-20:

> Speaking to yourselves in psalms and hymns and spiritual songs, singing and making melody in your heart to the Lord; Giving thanks always for all things unto God and the Father in the name of our Lord Jesus Christ.

Praying without ceasing involves an attitude of heart which says, in effect, "I am open that the Holy Spirit of God might at all times use me as a basis for making requests for those things that I or others need. Although I am not constantly thinking at all times about every given situation, I am open to this."

Praying in the Holy Ghost. Paul says to pray in the Holy Ghost. We must realize that the Holy Ghost is our helper. He is the one who has been sent for that purpose. We can therefore pray without ceasing because we realize that the work of God involves all of us. We then think of God's work in the world and we think of those with whom we have contact.

I pray that our prayer life will be strengthened as we meditate constantly on what has been discussed in this chapter.

Case Studies in Prayer

Instructions: Psalm 23 is an example of how one servant of the Lord "prayed without ceasing." The following exercises will lead you into an in-depth study of David's psalm.

The first seven exercises consist of a series of "discovery" questions, followed by a summary question. The eighth exercise asks you to summarize and apply the information you gained in the first seven exercises. The ninth exercise asks you to apply the wisdom you gained from this "case study in prayer" to your private prayer life.

A Psalm of David

The Lord is my shepherd, I shall not want. He maketh me to lie down in green pastures: he leadeth me beside the still waters. He restoreth my soul: he leadeth me in the paths of righteousness for his name's sake. Yea, though I walk through the valley of the shadow of death, I will fear no evil: for thou art with me; thy rod and thy staff they comfort me.

Thou preparest a table before me in the presence of mine enemies: thou anointest my head with oil; my cup runneth over. Surely goodness and mercy shall follow me all the days of my life: and I will dwell in the house of the Lord for ever. (Psalm 23)

1. David's Early Life

David's early life is reflected in Psalm 23.

a. Where was David born? (1 Samuel 16:1; 17:12)

b. How many brothers did David have? (16:10-11)

c. What special talents did David have? (16:18-23; 17:34-36)

d. What was David's earliest occupation? (16:11)

e. What was David's special calling? (16:1, 13)

f. Summary Question: Based on your answers to questions a-e above, describe David's early life. Then tell how his earlier life is reflected in Psalm 23.

2. Duties of David, the Shepherd

David's life as a shepherd is reflected in Psalm 23.

a. What did shepherds do in the morning? (John 10:1-5)

b. How did shepherds care for straying sheep? (Ezekiel 34:11-12; Luke 15:4)

c. How did shepherds supply water to the flock? (Genesis 29:1-3, 8, 10; Exodus 2:16)

d. What did shepherds do in the evening? (Jeremiah 33:12-13; Ezekiel 20:37)

e. What did good shepherds do at night? (Luke 2:8; Nahum 3:18)

f. How did shepherds respond to the young and feeble? (Isaiah 40:11; Genesis 33:1-2, 13-14)

g. Summary Question: Describe David's daily life as a shepherd. Then explain how his life as a shepherd is reflected in Psalm 23.

3. David, the Shepherd and Danger

The dangers of being a shepherd are reflected in Psalm 23.

a. How did weather conditions affect the daily lives of shepherds? (Genesis 31:38-41)

b. What type food did shepherds usually eat? (Amos 7:14; Luke 15:16; Matthew 3:4)

c. What types of animals posed serious threats? (1 Samuel 17:34; Isaiah 31:4; Jeremiah 5:6; Amos 3:12)

d. What types of human beings posed serious threats? (Genesis 31:38-39)

e. What were the shepherd's chief weapons against enemies? (1 Samuel 17:40; Psalm 23:4; Zechariah 11:17)

f. Summary Question: Describe some of the dangers facing shepherds as they carried out their duties. Then point out the references to these dangers that are found in Psalm 23.

4. David's Young Adulthood

   David's young adulthood is reflected in Psalm 23.

   a. What brought David into national attention? (1 Samuel 17:17—18:2)
   b. How did David get into the royal court? (1 Samuel 18:1-5)
   c. Who became David's closest friend? (1 Samuel 18:1)
   d. Who eventually became David's greatest enemy? (1 Samuel 18:6-12)
   e. Summary Question: Describe David's young adulthood. Then explain how his young adulthood is reflected in Psalm 23.

5. David, the Fugitive

   David's life as a fugitive is reflected in Psalm 23.

   a. Why did David flee Saul? (1 Samuel 18:11-12, 15, 28-29; 19:1-2, 10)
   b. What dangers did David face as a fugitive? (19:11, 19; 22:1-23; 24:7)
   c. What are some victories that David experienced as a fugitive? (22:1—24:7; 30)
   d. How did God eventually remove David's greatest enemy? (31:1-13)
   e. Summary Question: Summarize David's struggle against Saul and the outcome of this experience. Then tell how David's experience with Saul is reflected in Psalm 23.

6. David, the Ruler

   David's life as a ruler is reflected in Psalm 23.

   a. When David crossed the Philistine frontier, was he a lone fugitive? Explain. (1 Samuel 27:1-2)

b. Over what city did David become a ruler? (27:6)

c. Over what other territory did David eventually rule? (2 Samuel 2:7; 5:4-10)

d. Summary Questions: Summarize David's growth as a ruler. Then explain how his experiences as a ruler are reflected in Psalm 23.

7. David's Victories

David's many military victories are reflected in Psalm 23.

a. What did the Philistines probably think of David and his servants? (2 Samuel 21:15-22)

b. List some of the other people whom David defeated. (8:1-18; 12:26-31)

c. Who was David's famous son? (12:24)

d. Summary Question: Describe David's life as a military hero. Then tell how this aspect of his life is reflected in Psalm 23.

8. Summary Exercise: Considering the various aspects of David's life (covered in questions #1-7), and considering Dr. Banks' comments regarding praying without ceasing (covered earlier in this chapter), explain how Psalm 23 is an example of how David prayed without ceasing.

9. Application: Compare and contrast your life with that of David the shepherd, ruler and king. Note particularly:

a) your responsibilities (on your job, in the church, and in your family).

b) your role in relationship to the Black community.

c) how God can help you to face dangers and threats.

d) how God promises to deliver you from your enemies.

e) how God has "kept you within the flock."

Then outline ways in which you can follow David's example in "praying without ceasing."

CHAPTER TWO

Praying and Repenting

The following Scriptures reflect the importance of prayer and repentance.

from Scripture

Daniel 9:4 *And I prayed unto the Lord my God, and made my confession, and said, O Lord, the great and dreadful God, keeping the covenant and mercy to them that love him, and to them that keep his commandments;*
5 We have sinned, and have committed iniquity, and have done wickedly, and have rebelled, even by departing from the precepts and from thy judgments:
8 O Lord, to us belongeth confusion of face, to our kings, to our princes, and to our fathers, because we have sinned against thee.

2 Chronicles 7:13 *If I shut up heaven that there be no rain, or if I command the locusts to devour the land, or if I send pestilence among my people;*
14 If my people, which are called by my name, shall humble themselves, and pray, and seek my face, and turn from their wicked ways; then will I hear from heaven, and will forgive their sin, and will heal their land.

Psalm 109:1 *Hold not thy peace, O God of my praise;*
2 For the mouth of the wicked and the mouth of the deceitful are opened against me: they have spoken against me with a lying tongue.
3 They compassed me about also with words of hatred; and fought against me without a cause.
4 For my love they are my adversaries; but I give myself unto prayer.

Ephesians 6:10 *Finally, my brethren, be strong in the Lord, and in the power of his might.*

18 Praying always with all prayer and supplication in the Spirit, and watching thereunto with all perseverance and supplication for all saints;

Acts 6:4 *But we will give ourselves continually to prayer, and to the ministry of the word.*

Hebrews 4:16 *Let us therefore come boldly unto the throne of grace, that we may obtain mercy, and find grace to help in time of need.*

Scripture Discussion

Prayer is the soul's contact and communion with God. In prayer, we adore Him for all of His transcended excellences. We thank Him for all of His manifold mercies. We confess our sins and we petition Him for those things we desire that are consistent with His will. We do all of this in the name of our Lord Jesus Christ and for the glory to God.

A number of expressions relating to prayer occur throughout the Bible. Some of them are: "Call upon me and I will answer thee", "Men began to call upon the Lord", "Ask and it shall be given", "Cry unto the Lord", "Seek and ye shall find", "Knock and the door shall be opened" and, of course, the Apostle Paul tells us "Cast all your cares upon Him." Each of the above expressions suggests an attitude of the heart that should accompany prayer.

Prayer—the Soul's Sincere Expression to God. The elements of prayer are: worship, confession, thanksgiving, supplication and surrender. These elements should flow from the heart during the time of prayer and should be the basis of our relationship with God as we pray.

Basically, prayer means to be prostrate before. This should be our attitude as we lay hold onto God. Many hymns suggest what we have just noted about prayer. One hymn says that "Prayer is the soul's sincere desire, unuttered or expressed. It is a hidden fire that trembles in the breast." That hymn is in many of our hymnals. We do not sing it very often today. However, in the old days, we sang this hymn quite freely and frequently.

Someone has suggested that prayer is the Christian's vital breath—the Christian's native air. Prayer is an expression that God expects from us when we become Christians. It is a response to God's life that He has given to us.

Prayer—The Source of Life through the Spirit. When Paul asks the Galatian Christians, "Have you been brought to life through the Spirit? Are you going to be made perfect by the flesh?" (Galatians 3:3, paraphrased), he implies that if we're going to grow, we need to lay hold upon a resource and develop the life that has been given to us, and that has been promised through prayer.

In prayer we receive light through the Spirit. We receive strength for the soul. We receive provision for the body and direction for every area of our lives. Prayer was important in the life of Jesus Christ. He is our model. In the Gospels, Jesus is seen very often in prayer.

Prayer is the most vital duty of a Christian. Prayer is not only a duty, but a privilege. Hebrews 4:16 says that we should come boldly to the throne of grace. It should be a privilege to come before God. It should be a privilege to have communion with Him. Prayer is important for that reason. Our life depends on it.

Prayer—The Most Important Task. If Satan's strategy is to be defeated, it must be through prayer. According to Ephesians 6:10, 18 the work of the Lord depends upon it. We must pray regarding the work that God has given us to do. It is a subject that we certainly cannot over-emphasize, as we look at the blessed Word of God. As we think of praying, we think of being totally dependent upon God.

In Acts 6:2, the apostles called the multitudes of disciples together, and the people laid before the apostles a need. However, the apostles said that they should not leave the Word of God and serve this particular need.

This physical activity (which had to do with distributing food to those who were hungry) was an important responsibility. Yet the apostles said it was not proper for the apostles themselves to leave the ministry of the Word of God. They said that they should give themselves unto prayer and to the ministry of the Word.

In a system of priorities such as these, the apostles realized their responsibilities before God, but said "we will give ourselves continually to prayer," realizing, of course, the necessity of praying. They wanted full lives. So they said, first of all, "We'll pray and then we'll administer the Word."

David, in the Old Testament had the same thought and expressed it in Psalm 109. He says throughout this passage, "I will give myself unto prayer. I will really become a praying person." David was praying about some problems that he had with his enemies. He said he would continually pray for them, although they sought to defeat him. Although his enemies sought to disturb his equilibrium, David gave himself to prayer.

Someone has said, "We can do nothing until we have prayed." After praying, that is all we can do. There is a ministry of prayer.

Prayer—The Means of Repenting. In prayer we make a covenant with God to repent of our sins. There is no possibility of our getting through to God and there is no assurance that He will hear or answer if we have not repented.

In the Sermon on the Mount, the Lord said to those who bring Him gifts, "If you bring your gift to the altar, and there remember that your brother has aught against you. Leave the gift, and go and make things right with your brother and come and offer your gifts" (Matthew 5:23, 24, paraphrased). Confession and repentance are vital necessities if we are going to be good and praying people.

The Bible also says that we should confess to the one sinned against as well as to God. The Lord said that we should go and make things right with our brother and then come back to Him with our gifts.

What are some of the things that should accompany prayer? To answer this question, we must go through the Word of God and seek the elements and the aspects of prayer that are presented there.

Prayer—An Expression of Humility. We are all familiar with 2 Chronicles 7:14. In fact, it's one of the most often quoted verses when it comes to the matter of prayer. This verse calls for repentance from sin and deep humility. That, of course, is what is involved in being "prostrate before," in mind as well as body.

There needs to be a right relationship with God. What is a right relationship with God? 1 Samuel 7:3-4 provides an example.

> If ye do return unto the Lord with all your hearts, then put away the strange gods and Ashtaroth from among you, and prepare your hearts unto the Lord, and serve him only: and he will deliver you out of the hand of the Philistines. Then the children of Israel did put away Baalim and Ashtaroth, and served the Lord only.

Here we see the House of Israel putting away the idols that had occupied their time and attention and that they had substituted for the worship of God. This Scripture indicates there are those things that we need to lay aside if we are going to be in a right relationship with God.

It also illustrates that confession of sin is a vital necessity if we are going to pray. 1 John 1:9 tells us that, "If we confess our sins, he is faithful and just to forgive us...and to cleanse us from all unrighteousness."

When praying for his people, Daniel also emphasized confession of sins. In Daniel 9:4-19, we find that confession of sins is a vital necessity if we are going to pray.

May the Lord impress on us the importance of what has been mentioned in this chapter about preparations for prayer. We must not disregard these principles, feeling that we can get through to the Lord anyway. In our hearts and minds, let us be sure that we prepare for communion with God.

Case Studies in Prayer

Instructions: Jacob's prayer provides a good example of what Dr. Banks considered the importance of repentance in prayer. The following exercises will lead you into an in-depth study of Jacob's prayer. The first four exercises consist of a series of "discovery" questions, followed by a summary question. The fifth exercise asks you to summarize and apply the information you gained in the first four exercises. The sixth exercise asks you to apply the wisdom you gained from this "case study in prayer" to your private prayer life.

Jacob's Prayer of Repentance

> And Jacob said, O God of my father Abraham, and God of my father Isaac, the Lord which saidst unto me, Return unto thy country, and to thy kindred, and I will deal well with thee: I am not worthy of the least of all the mercies, and of all the truth, which thou has shown unto thy servant; for with my staff I passed over this Jordan;

and now I am become two bands.

Deliver me, I pray thee, from the hand of my brother, from the hand of Esau: for I fear him, lest he will come and smite me, and the mother with the children. And thou saidst, I will surely do thee good, and make thy seed as the sand of the sea, which cannot be numbered for multitude....

And Jacob was left alone; and there wrestled a man with him until the breaking of the day. And when he saw that he prevailed not against him, he touched the hollow of his thigh; and the hollow of Jacob's thigh was out of joint, as he wrestled with him.

And he said, Let me go, for the day breaketh. And he said, I will not let thee go, except thou bless me. And he said unto him, What is thy name? And he said, Jacob. And he said, Thy name shall be called no more Jacob, but Israel: for as a prince hast thou power with God and with men, and hast prevailed.

And Jacob asked him, and said, Tell me, I pray thee, thy name. And he said, Wherefore is it that thou dost ask after my name? And he blessed him there. And Jacob called the name of the place Peniel: for I have seen God face to face, and my life is preserved. (Genesis 32:9-12, 24-30)

1. Jacob's Early Life

Jacob refers to his early life in his prayer.

a. Who were Jacob's parents? (Genesis 25:21-26)

b. What was unusual about Jacob's birth? (25:21-26)

c. Where did Jacob grow up? (25:18)

On what continent was the country where Jacob grew up?

d. Which parent favored Jacob most? (25:28)

e. What parent favored Esau most? (25:28)

f. To what does a birthright entitle a firstborn son? (Deuteronomy 21:17; Genesis 27:27-29; 28:4)

g. Who (Jacob or Esau) was to get the birthright, and why? (25:26-28)

h. Summary Question: Considering the informa tion provided in questions a-g, explain what it was that God had asked Jacob to do, and Jacob hadn't done. (32:9)

2. Jacob's Sin

Jacob referred to specific sins in his prayer.

a. How did Jacob get Esau to sell his birthright? (Genesis 25:27-34)

b. What did Jacob pay for Esau's birthright? (25:29-34)

c. What did Jacob gain from the birthright? (27:22-28, 36-37)

d. How was it that Jacob received a second blessing from Isaac? (27:41—28:5)

e. Why did Jacob flee his homeland? (27:41—28:5)

f. Summary Question: Considering your answers to questions a-e, explain what Jacob means when he says that he is not worthy of God's mercies. (32:10)

3. Jacob's Previous Encounter with God

Jacob refers to previous encounters with God in his

prayer.

a. Where was Jacob when he had his "ladder dream"? (Genesis 28:10-12)

b. Describe Jacob's dream. (28:12-16)

c. What had God promised Jacob? (28:13-16)

d. What had Jacob promised God? (28:20-22)

e. Summary Question: Summarize the circumstances and content of Jacob's dream. Then explain what Jacob means when, in his later prayer of repentance, he reminds God of God's previous promises to him. (32:12)

4. Jacob's Life Becomes Complicated

Stress from a complicated life is reflected in Jacob's prayer.

a. Who was Laban? (Genesis 28:2-5; 24:15, 28)

b. When did conflict between Laban and Jacob begin developing? (29:13-29)

c. In what ways were Jacob and Laban somewhat alike? (27:36; 29:13-29)

d. How did Jacob come to have children by four different women? (29:1—30:24)

e. What grievances did Jacob have against Laban? (30:25—31:6)

f. How did Jacob's entire family get involved? (30:25—31:55)

g. How was the conflict between Laban and Jacob finally resolved? (31:36-55)

h. As soon as Jacob resolved his differences with Laban, what other problems developed? (32:1-8) What are the two bands? (32:7)

i. What strategies did Jacob use to resolve his conflict with Esau? (32:13-23)

j. Summary Question: Considering the answers to questions a-i, explain some of the sins that had "caught up with" Jacob and how this might have contributed to his emotional state when he first cried out in repentance. (32:11) Also explain how these problems might have led to his "wrestling match" with God and his second prayer. (32:24-30)

5. Summary Exercise: Consider the outcomes of Jacob's struggle with God (32:29—33:20). Then explain how Jacob's story is an example of 2 Chronicles 7:13, mentioned by Dr. Banks earlier in this chapter.

6. Application: Think of your relationships with other people. Are there ways in which you have wronged others? If so, follow Jacob's example and first repent before the Lord. Then resolve your conflict with your brother or sister.

CHAPTER THREE

Putting On God's Armor

These Scriptures from Ephesians emphasize the realities of spiritual warfare.

from Scripture
Ephesians 6:10 *Finally, my brethren, be strong in the Lord, and in the power of his might.*
11 Put on the whole armour of God, that ye may be able to stand against the wiles of the devil.
12 For we wrestle not against flesh and blood, but against principalities, against powers, against the rulers of the darkness of this world, against spiritual wickedness in high places.
13 Wherefore take unto you the whole armour of God, that ye may be able to withstand in the evil day, and having done all, to stand.
14 Stand therefore, having your loins girt about with truth, and having on the breastplate of righteousness;
15 And your feet shod with the preparation of the gospel of peace;
16 Above all, taking the shield of faith, wherewith ye shall be able to quench all the fiery darts of the wicked.
17 And take the helmet of salvation, and the sword of the Spirit, which is the word of God:
18 Praying always with all prayer and supplication in the Spirit, and watching thereunto with all perseverance and supplication for all saints.

Scripture Discussion

In the book, *The Power of Prayer and the Prayer of Power,*[1] R. A. Torrey refers to Ephesians 6:18. This verse indicates that the intelligent child of God should be given to prayer. The child of God must pray, pray, pray.

The children of God must pray in order to put enemies out of their hearts and in order to put all of their hearts into prayer. Whatever else we do, we must pray.

The Need for God's Armor. Of course, the Holy Spirit is also involved. This is what Paul means when he says, in Romans 8, that the Spirit prays through us. Knowing who we are approaching is part of preparing for prayer.

Prayer, many times, is a spontaneous expression from our hearts. However, sometimes there are serious and critical issues before us that demand a bit more energy and a bit more intensity. Recall that our Lord Jesus Christ in the Garden of Gethsemane shed great drops of blood.

Girding the Loins. Preparation requires taking the whole armor of God and this armor is many faceted. One part of the armor is having our loins "girt about with truth" (Ephesians 6:14). We know that if we pray according to God's will, God will hear us (1 John 5:14). Therefore, if we are going to pray according to His will, we must know His will. To know His will, we must enter intelligently into what God has to say.

The Lord Jesus Christ assures us that we should pray in His name (John 16:23, 24). Praying in His name can have tremendous results.

The Breastplate of Righteousness. The second part of the armor that we must have is righteousness. The Bible says that we should have our loins girded about with truth, but we should also have on the breastplate of righteousness. The expression, "breastplate of righteousness" (Ephesians 6:14) stands for the thing that is apparent to men, to God, and to us as we go forth to battle.

The righteousness in our hearts and in our minds should be displayed not self-righteously, but in a godly and righteous manner.

The breastplate is used as a shield for the body. The breastplate of righteousness relates to the spiritual man. This breastplate sustains and protects.

The Shodding of the Feet. Ephesians 6:15 indicates that our feet should be shod "with the preparation of the gospel of peace." This, of course, is our entree to people as we walk in the world. We cannot go promoting any other philosophy. We can't go promoting ourselves. It must be that we're looking forward to promoting Christ who is the heart, substance and source of the Gospel. Jesus Christ is the message. This thought has to be in our hearts and minds. It has to be in our hearts when we pray.

The Shield of Faith. The shield of faith, mentioned in Ephesians 6:16 is a very colorful picture of how, in all circumstances and in any situation we must reflect the great dependency we have upon God. David illustrates this when he was faced with Goliath. In what may have seemed to be reckless abandon, David came toward the giant with just some smooth stones and a sling. Here is a great demonstration of one who took the shield of faith that the Apostle Paul describes. David said to Goliath, "Thou comest to me with a sword, and with a spear, and with a shield: but I come to thee in the name of the Lord of hosts, the God of the armies of Israel, whom thou hast defied." (1 Samuel 17:45) David's faith rested strong in God and in his relationship to God.

The Helmet of Salvation. In Ephesians 6:17 the Apostle Paul says to take the helmet of salvation and the sword of the spirit. The helmet of salvation is something that would crown one's head. It covers the head when necessary. The head symbolizes a sense of direction. The head stands for what is involved in having knowledge about a situation we face.

The Sword of the Spirit. (Ephesians 6:17) The sword of the Spirit is that which the Holy Spirit has given. It is that which the Holy Spirit uses through us to take care of our needs. We know that there is no greater weapon that can be used as we go forth than the sword of the Spirit, the Word of God.

The Lord Jesus used this sword as He was tempted of Satan on the mountain, prior to His public ministry (Matthew 4:1-11). We are told that He overcame with the Word of God–"it is written" (v. 10). We can carry that example of Christ as we go forth.

The "Proper Gear." After making all of the above preparation for battle, the Apostle Paul says, in Ephesians 6:18, that we should always pray. This suggests that, through proper conditioning of the heart and mind, our total being should be in "proper gear," and in a proper relationship with God. We should be "honed" as if we were a sword. With all of this preparation, we can concentrate on the battle before us.

The Apostle Paul also presents an energetic prayer life when he says, in Ephesians 6, that we need to put on the whole armor of God, that we might be able to stand against the wiles of the devil. Here we are praying because our enemy has employed various devices against us. This is all the more reason that preparation for prayer is vital and necessary.

In Ephesians 6:12, Paul points out that we wrestle not against flesh and blood. It is not against other human beings that we fight. It is against principalities and powers—spiritual wickedness. These are the things that make both preparation and a vital sensitivity to the idea of prayer important. Prayer for the persons with whom we are involved is vitally necessary.

The "All's." The Apostle Paul presents a number of ideas about prayer. In Ephesians a number of these ideas are presented. One can learn quite a bit about prayer by studying carefully many of the phrases in Ephesians 6 which begin with "all."

These include: "all prayer", "all saints", "all supplication", "all seasons in the Spirit", "all perseverance", and "for all saints". In considering prayer, we should study and meditate upon each of these phrases. In fact, we need to give emphasis to them in our daily lives. These words are vital for our understanding of prayer and for our understanding of the prayer life.

The "Watch." Notice that Paul said, "watch" also (Ephesians 6:18). Torrey comments that this has to do with being sleepless. The idea of watching, of course, is there because we have a tendency to fall asleep when we pray. This is why we need to keep Ephesians 6 in mind.

Torrey says that Paul realized the natural slothfulness of man and especially man's natural slothfulness in prayer. Most of us, of course, would readily agree that prayer is an area where we easily get drowsy or fall asleep. For this reason, Torrey mentions, we seldom pray through. Therefore we should be careful.

How often do we as a church and as individuals, in the midst of what might be a blessing from God, get drowsy or quit? Considering this tendency toward drowsiness, when it comes to prayer, we can see the importance of watching when we pray.

Other Injunctions Regarding Prayer. Notice that Ephesians 6:10-17 carry many injunctions about prayer. First of all, we are told that we must prepare for the warfare in which Christians are engaged. In the last three verses, we see that prayer is vital in this warfare and it is vital for the victory that we seek.

There also needs to be preparation for prayer. There needs to be a sensing in our minds, hearts and spirits of the Person to whom we are praying and of the Person in whose energy we come. It is to the throne of God the Father that we come. It is our Lord and Saviour Jesus Christ who is our Intercessor. He is the one who makes acceptable the words that we speak.

May God continue to guide our thinking as we prepare to enter into communion with Him.

1. R. A. Torrey, *The Power of Prayer and the Prayer of Power* (Grand Rapids: Zondervan Publishing House, 1955).

Case Studies in Prayer

Instructions: Below is a prayer that Moses and the Children of Israel sang to the Lord after He delivered them from Egypt through the Red Sea. The following exercises will lead you into an in-depth study of this prayer.

Each of the first five exercises consists of a series of "discovery" questions, followed by a summary question. The sixth exercise asks for a summary and an application. The seventh exercise asks you to apply the wisdom you gained from this "case study in prayer" to your private prayer life.

A Prayer of Moses and the Children of Israel

> Then sang Moses and the children of Israel this song unto the Lord, and spake, saying, I will sing unto the LORD, for he hath triumphed gloriously: the horse and his rider hath he thrown into the sea. The LORD is my strength and song, and he is become my salvation: he is my God, and I will prepare him an habitation; my father's God, and I will exalt him.

> The LORD is a man of war: the LORD is his name. Pharaoh's chariots and his host hath he cast into the sea: his chosen captains also are drowned in the Red sea...Thy right hand, O LORD, is become glorious in power: thy right hand, O LORD, hath dashed in pieces the enemy...
>
> The enemy said, I will pursue, I will overtake, I will divide the spoil; my lust shall be satisfied upon them; I will draw my sword, my hand shall destroy them. Thou didst blow with thy wind, the sea covered them: they sank as lead in the mighty waters. Who is like unto thee, O LORD, among the gods? who is like thee, glorious in holiness, fearful in praises, doing wonders?...
>
> And Miriam the prophetess, the sister of Aaron, took a timbrel in her hand; and all the women went out after her with timbrels and with dances. And Miriam answered them, Sing ye to the LORD, for he hath triumphed gloriously; the horse and his rider hath he thrown into the sea. (Exodus 15:1-4, 6, 9-11, 20-21)

1. Moses' Early Life

To Moses, this prayer also refers to his early life.

a. Who was Moses' father? (Exodus 2:1)

b. Who was Moses' mother? (2:1)

c. Moses was a member of what group of people? (2:1, 2)

d. When Moses was born, where were the Israelites and what was their plight? (1:5-14)

e. Why did Moses' mother have to hide him? (1:15-22)

f. How did Moses happen to become a part of Pharaoh's household? (2:1-10)

g. How did Moses become separated from Pharaoh's household? (2:11-15)

h. Summary Question: Outline the birth, early childhood and early adulthood of Moses. Then explain how many of the references in the prayer of praise might also be made of Moses' early life.

2. Moses' Special Calling

Moses had a special role in the lives of the Israelites.

a. What did God call Moses to do? (Exodus 3:1-12)

b. How did Pharaoh respond when Aaron and Moses approached him concerning freedom of the Children of Israel? (5:1-7)

c. Describe some of the plagues that God brought on Pharaoh and the Egyptians. (7:20-21; 8:5-7, 16, 20-24; 11:1-5)

d. What made Pharaoh let the Children of Israel go? (12:12-13, 29-33)

e. Once Pharaoh let the Children of Israel go, what did he do? (14:5-9)

f. Summary Question: Give an overview of the situation that led up to the confrontation between Pharaoh and the Children of Israel at the Red Sea. Then point out references to the confrontation in the above quoted prayer of praise.

3. God's Deliverance

The Children of Israel sang about their deliverance from Egypt.

a. How did the Children of Israel feel when they saw Pharaoh and his army coming after them? (Exodus

14:11-12)

b. What did Moses tell the people at the Red Sea? (14:13-14)

c. What did God say to Moses at the Red Sea? (14:15-18)

d. What happened to Pharaoh and his army when they went after the Children of Israel? (14:19-30)

e. How did the Children of Israel respond to this? (14:31)

f. Summary Question: Describe how the Lord delivered the Children of Israel from Pharaoh and the Egyptians. Then point out references of it in the above prayer of praise.

4. The Sword

The Children of Israel sang about the sword of the Lord.

a. With what is a sword usually associated? (Leviticus 26:25; Isaiah 34:5)

b. In some parts of Scripture, the sword is used to illustrate how what works? (Ephesians 6:17; Hebrews 4:12)

c. In other sections of Scripture, who is the "sword"? (Isaiah 49:2; Revelation 1:16)

d. Considering a, b & c above, what does Ephesians 6:17 mean when it refers to the "sword" of the Spirit?

e. Summary Question: Review your answers to questions a-d. Then compare and contrast the sword of Pharaoh (or Satan) with the sword of the Spirit. (Exodus 15:9; Ephesians 6:17)

5. The Shield

A shield is another weapon of war that has special

spiritual meaning.

a. What is one thing that the term "shield" symbolizes? (Genesis 15:1; Deuteronomy 33:29; 2 Samuel 22:3; Psalm 3:3; 5:12)

b. What is another thing that the term "shield" sometimes symbolizes? (Psalm 91:4)

c. What is another thing that the term "shield" sometimes symbolizes? (2 Samuel 22:36; Psalm 18:35)

d. What is yet another thing that the term "shield" is used to illustrate? (Ephesians 6:16)

e. Summary Question: Using as background, the Scriptures studied in a-d, summarize various meanings of the term "shield" in the Word of God. Then, from the prayer of praise (quoted above) point out the ways in which the Lord acted as a shield for the Children of Israel.

6. Summary Exercise: Reflect on the history of Black America. Identify specific forces of evil which have attempted to destroy it. Explain how God delivered. Then recall "prayers of praise" (such as "You know, I love the Lord. He heard my cry") which Black Americans have sung. Compare and contrast some of these songs with the prayer of praise (quoted above).

7. Application: Think of a personal struggle that you have had, involving a particular force of evil. Then take time to sing or whisper a prayer of praise to the Lord.

CHAPTER FOUR

Praying with Purpose

Jesus emphasized the importance of praying with purpose and with sincerity.

from Scripture
Hebrews 7:25 *Wherefore he is able also to save them to the uttermost that come unto God by him, seeing he ever liveth to make intercession for them.*
Romans 8:34 *Who is he that condemneth? It is Christ that died, yea rather, that is risen again, who is even at the right hand of God, who also maketh intercession for us.*
James 4:1 *From whence come wars and fightings among you? come they not hence, even of your lusts that war in your members?*
2 Ye lust, and have not: ye kill, and desire to have, and cannot obtain: ye fight and war, yet ye have not, because ye ask not.
John 16:24 *Hitherto have ye asked nothing in my name: ask, and ye shall receive, that your joy may be full.*

Scripture Discussion

R.A. Torrey, in his book, *The Power of Prayer and the Prayer of Power,* includes a very timely and well-worded poem about prayer.

> I met God in the morning, when the day was at its best. And his presence came like sunrise, like a Glory in my breast. All day long His presence lingered; all day long he

stayed with me. And I sailed in perfect calmness, over a very troubled sea.

Other ships were blown and battered; Other ships were sore distressed. But the winds that seemed to drive them, brought to us a perfect rest.

Then I thought of stormy mornings, with a keen remorse of mind; When I too had loosed the moorings with thy presence left behind.

So I think I know the secret, learned from many a troubled days. You must seek Him in the morning, if you want Him throughout the day.[1]

This poem quoted by Torrey, is a very timely and well-worded comment on prayer. Let's focus on why Torrey says prayer is so vitally important in the Christian life.

Prayer in the Life of Christ. One reason that we need to have persistent, constant, sleepless, overcoming prayer is that prayer occupied a very prominent place in the life of our Lord Jesus Christ, both on earth and in heaven. In Scripture Christ is seen rising and praying before day and going out in the evening and praying. In some instances, He prayed all night. If our Lord Jesus, who is our model, sees the need for prayer, we too must see the need for it in our daily lives.

Prayer was not only an earthly part of Jesus' ministry, it is also a vital part of His present ministry. Hebrews 7:25 says that our Lord is able to save to the utmost anyone who comes to Him. We see Him living forever to make intercession for us. The Lord Jesus Christ engages in intercessory prayer.

His prayer is the same as our prayer should be for those with whom we are in contact. He prays for us. We pray to God through Him and He makes that prayer request acceptable.

Romans 8:34 gives us more information about Jesus Christ, our Intercessor. The Lord Jesus Christ was crucified, buried, and was raised again from the dead on the third day. However, He didn't stay on earth. He was here for only a period of time.

He went back to heaven because it was vitally necessary that He be at the right hand of the Father to make intercession for us. He's not there necessarily because He's the Son of God. He's always been in control of the universe.

He returned there in order that He might through that ministry of prayer, intercede for us.

It is a wonderful thought—a thought so wonderful and comforting—to realize that Jesus Christ hastened back to the throne of God that He might intercede for us. Therefore, we can come to God through Him. Isn't it wonderful to realize this?

Pray for Protection from the Adversary. First of all, prayer is needful because there is a devil. There is a real enemy. We are not wrestling against flesh and blood. We are wrestling against a very intelligent foe. We need to be aware of that. Prayer is necessary because there is a real devil, a real adversary. Why should we pray? We should pray for protection from the devil.

Pray that God Makes You an Intercessor. Desire to have fellowship with Jesus Christ to that end. Tell the Father that whatever else He may make you, make you, at all times, an intercessor. Desire that He makes you a person who knows how to pray and spends much time in prayer.

Pray for Mercy and Grace. Another reason that constant, persistent, sleepless and overcoming prayer is important is that prayer is the means God has appointed for receiving mercy and for obtaining grace to help in the time of need. Some may say they thought these things were automatically there because God has promised them. Yes they are.

However, sensitivity to them and enjoyment of them comes as we lay claim to them. We must appropriate them. It is the same as having a sum of money in the bank. We know it is there. On any day, we can present our bank books and we can testify to the fact that our money is there.

However, the money is only available for us to use, if we write a check or make out the proper withdrawal form, so that we can have the money in our hands and in our pockets.

It is the same with blessings that God has at His disposal for us. We must come boldly to the Throne of grace to obtain God's resources for us. As we approach God in bold and confident prayer, God dispenses His grace and mercy to us.

As Torrey says, mercy is what we need. We also need grace. Grace is what we must have or all our life's effort will be a complete failure. Prayer is the way to get the grace and mercy that we need.

Pray for Fullness of Joy. There's a seventh reason that we must pray. It is to obtain fullness of joy. Praying in the name of Jesus is the way Jesus Christ Himself told His disciples to obtain fullness of joy. It is by asking in the name of Jesus that we receive fullness of joy. John 16:24 is very clear about this.

Certainly we want to be joyful believers. We want to be joyful Christians. We want to exude that glow from within as we approach others, and as we come face to face with situations and circumstances. The way for that to take place is for us to realize that the fullness of joy is in Jesus Christ. The Lord said to ask for it in His name.

The Lord Jesus was able to exude radiance and evidence of victory in His life and work. This is because He was in contact with God. As a result, God gave Him the glow and confidence He needed to have throughout His life. We can receive the same glow if we follow Jesus Christ's example.

Pray to Obtain God's Blessings. Torrey says prayer is important because it is God's appointed way for obtaining things. God has said that all things are available to us through prayer. It is through prayer that God makes available to us all of the resources we need and all the things that He promises.

James highlights this by saying that we do not have things because we do not ask for them (James 4:2). This statement may seem simple, but we can accept it from the Word of God. Prayer is the way that God designed that we get things.

Pray to Move Forward. In his commentary on prayer, Torrey asks several questions and then answers them by pointing up the need for prayer. First of all, he asks why many Christians lack progress in their Christian lives. It is because they neglect to pray. Why is it that many ministers find no fruit in their labor? It is because they have not been prayerful.

Why do Sunday School teachers fail to see fruit in their Sunday School classes? It is because of a lack of prayer. Why do ministers and churches say they are making so little headway? The answer, again, is a lack of prayer.

God has said that He will unleash the resources we need, if we pray. Now that we have stated some major reasons for praying, we will focus on the need to pray with sincerity.

Avoid Vain Repetitions! In Matthew 6:6-8, our Lord gives some guidelines for praying. Most of the guidelines concern avoiding practices that are typical of hypocrites. For example, He says that we should avoid vain repetition. In this way we do not pray in order to be heard by other people.

He says that the hypocrites of His day often stood on corners of streets so that they could be seen and heard praying. They also wanted to be rewarded through the praises of others. Our Lord tells us not to be like that. Vain repetitions and babblings have no strength in themselves. They do not really come out of the heart, but are merely from the lips. They do not prepare one for meaningful communication with God.

Go into Your Closet. Our Lord suggested that when we pray, we enter into our "closets." Instead of being ostentatious, we should seek our Father in secret. Our Father will reward us openly.

The secret place should first of all, be in our hearts. Diligent search has to do with being in a quiet, secret place with God. The Psalmist in Psalm 91:1 heralded this fact when he said that "He that dwelleth in the secret place of the most High shall abide under the shadow of the Almighty."

In summary, when we pray, we need to pray with purpose and sincerity. Among the purposes for praying are: praying for protection from the adversary, praying that God makes us intercessors, praying to obtain God's blessings, praying to move forward, praying for mercy and grace, and praying for fullness of joy.

May God enable us to do just that!

R. A. Torrey, *The Power of Prayer and the Prayer of Power* (Grand Rapids: Zondervan Publishing House, 1955).

Case Studies in Prayer

Instructions: The following exercises will lead you into an in-depth study of the Lord's Prayer. Each of the first seven exercises consists of a series of "discovery" questions, followed by a summary question. The eighth exercise asks for a summary and an application.

The ninth exercise asks you to apply the wisdom you gained from this "case study in prayer" to your private prayer life.

The Lord's Prayer

> After this manner therefore pray ye: Our Father which art in heaven, Hallowed be thy name. Thy kingdom come. Thy will be done in earth, as it is in heaven. Give us this day our daily bread. And forgive us our debts, as we forgive our debtors.
>
> And lead us not into temptation, but deliver us from evil: For thine is the kingdom, and the power, and the glory, for ever. Amen. (Matthew 6:9-13)

1. "Our Father which art in heaven..."

   The Lord's Prayer focuses on God the Father.

   a. What relationship does God the Father have with Jesus Christ? (Ephesians 1:17; 1 Corinthians 8:6)

   b. What relationship did God the Father have to the Jewish nation? (Deuteronomy 32:6; Hosea 11:1; Psalm 103:13)

   c. What relationship does God the Father have with the things that He created? (James 1:17; Hebrews 12:9)

   d. What relationship is God the Father to humankind? (Acts 7:26)

   e. What relationship is there between God the Father and His saved and redeemed people? (John 1:12; 3:16; Luke 15:11-32; Romans 8:14-16)

f. In what ways is God similar to earthly fathers? (Hebrews 12:5-11)

g. Summary Question: Dr. Banks suggests that we emulate Christ in prayer. Considering your answers to questions a-f, what does the first sentence of the Lord's Prayer suggest about how we should approach our heavenly Father in prayer?

2. "Hallowed be thy name..."

Draft a definition of the term "hallowed" from the following Scriptures.

a. Isaiah 65:5

b. John 17:19; 10:36; Galatians 1:15

c. Exodus 29:36; Leviticus 8:15; Numbers 7:1; 1 Kings 8:64

d. Exodus 20:8

e. Acts 20:32

f. Summary Question: What does the term "hallowed" mean when applied to God's name? If we are to emulate Christ, as Dr. Banks recommends, what does the phrase "Hallowed be thy name" indicate about our approach to God?

3. "Thy kingdom come, Thy will be done..."

Many passages of Scripture speak of the kingdom of heaven.

a. Describe Isaiah's vision of the heavenly kingdom. (Isaiah 65:17-25)

b. Describe Jeremiah's vision of the heavenly kingdom. (Jeremiah 31:27-34)

c. Describe John the Apostle's vision of the heavenly kingdom. (Revelation 21:1-5)

d. Describe the Apostle Peter's vision of the heavenly

kingdom. (2 Peter 3:10-13)

e. How does Jesus Christ Himself describe the heavenly kingdom? (Matthew 8:10-12; 24:44, 50, 51; 25:31-46)

f. How do some of the parables describe the kingdom of heaven? (Matthew 13:24-30, 33, 36-43, 47-50; Luke 13:18-21)

g. Summary Question: Describe the "Kingdom" (of heaven or of God) as it is presented in Scripture. Then, in your opinion, explain why the phrase, "Thy will be done" follows the phrase "Thy kingdom come". If we are to emulate Christ, as Dr. Banks recommends, what do these two phrases suggest regarding our attitude toward God in prayer?

4. "Give us this day our daily bread..."

Bread is a symbol that appears throughout the Word of God.

What does the word "bread" symbolize in each of the following Scriptures?

a. 1 Kings 22:27; Isaiah 30:20

b. Psalm 127:2

c. Psalm 80:5

d. Proverbs 4:17

e. Proverbs 20:17

f. Exodus 16:14-36; Numbers 11:5-9

g. John 6:47-58; Matthew 4:4

h. Summary Question: Dr. Banks suggests that we emulate Christ in prayer. Considering this, substitute some of the various meanings for "bread" (from questions a-g) into the phrase "Give us this day our daily bread". Then explain what this phrase suggests about our attitude toward God in prayer.

5. "And forgive us our debts as we forgive our debtors..."

The Lord's Prayer makes a reference to debt.

a. What were the basic arrangements between debtors and debtees in the Mosaic Law? (Deuteronomy 15:2-11; Psalm 37:25-26; Matthew 5:42)

b. How was usury generally viewed? (Proverbs 28:8; Ezekiel 18:8, 17)

c. What were some of the regulations regarding how a debtor could approach a debtee? (Deuteronomy 15:1-15; 24:10-13; Job 22:6; 24:7-9)

d. What measures could be taken against debtees? (Leviticus 25:23-41)

e. Summary Question: God designed the Mosaic Laws regarding debtors. With this in mind, and using as background, the Scriptures studied in a-d, consider our relationship to God. In what sense are we indebted to Him? In what sense is He a compassionate debtor? If we are to emulate Christ, as Dr. Banks suggests, what does the phrase "Forgive us our debts as we forgive our debtors..." suggest about our attitude toward God in prayer and our attitudes toward others?

6. "Lead us not into temptation, but deliver us from evil..."

The struggle with temptation is one of the greatest battles of the Christian life.

a. From where do many temptations come? (Matthew 26:40; Romans 8:3-6; 2 Corinthians 7:5; Galatians 5:16; Ephesians 2:3; James 1:13-15)

b. Who is another great tempter? (1 Corinthians 7:5; 1 Thessalonians 3:5; Revelation 12:9; Matthew 4:3)

c. What is yet another source of temptation? (Genesis 39:7-9; 1 Kings 10:1; Daniel 1:11-14; Matthew 16:1; 19:3; 22:18)

d. What can we learn from Satan's temptation of our Lord Jesus Christ? (Matthew 4:1-11; Mark 1:12-13; Luke 4:1-13; 22:28; Hebrews 4:15)

e. What can we learn from God's restriction of Satan's power in the temptation of Job? (Job 1:1-12)

f. Summary Question: Consider your answers to questions a-e. If we are to emulate Christ, as Dr. Banks recommends, what does the phrase "Lead us not into temptation but deliver us from evil" suggest about things for which we should petition God?

7. "For thine is the kingdom, and the power, and the glory for ever. Amen."

Many prophecies say that our Lord will establish the kingdom of heaven on earth one day.

a. What is the kingdom of heaven? (John 3:18; Matthew 13:24-30, 36-43, 47-50)

b. What are two types of power at work in the life of the Christian? (Genesis 31:6; Psalm 22:20; Isaiah 37:27; John 1:12; Acts 5:4; 1 Corinthians 7:37; 9:4; Matthew 28:18-20)

c. What does the term "glory" mean? (Exodus 33:17-20; 16:5-10; John 1:14-17; 2:11; 2 Peter 1:17)

d. What do God, the kingdom of God and the children of God have in common? (Psalm 90:1-2; 102:24-28; Isaiah 57:15; 44:6-8; 1 Timothy 6:16; 2 Peter 3:7-13; Revelation 1:4-7)

e. Summary Question: Using information gained in questions a-d, explain what the final sentence of the Lord's Prayer suggests about the content of our prayers.

8. Summary Exercise: Review Dr. Banks' recommendations regarding emulating Christ in prayer. Then explain the ways in which the "Lord's Prayer" is an example of a prayer which: a) prays for protection from the adversary, b) intercedes for others, c) asks for mercy and grace, d) brings fullness of joy, e) seeks God's blessings and, f) asks for power to move forward.

9. Application: Review the information from questions #1-7. Then create a "checklist" of things to pray about and ways that we should approach God in prayer. Occasionally review this checklist as you approach the Lord each day. Pray that God will use the checklist to improve your personal communication with Him.

CHAPTER FIVE

Surrendering to God

Through physical postures we tell the Lord that we surrender to Him.

from Scripture

1 Timothy 2:8 *I will therefore that men pray every where, lifting up holy hands, without wrath and doubting.*

Ephesians 3:14 *For this cause I bow my knees unto the Father of our Lord Jesus Christ,*

15 Of whom the whole family in heaven and earth is named,

16 That he would grant you, according to the riches of his glory, to be strengthened with might by his Spirit in the inner man;

17 That Christ may dwell in your hearts by faith; that ye, being rooted and grounded in love,

18 May be able to comprehend with all saints what is the breadth, and length, and depth, and height;

19 And to know the love of Christ, which passeth knowledge, that ye might be filled with all the fulness of God.

Psalm 6:6 *I am weary with my groaning; all the night make I my bed to swim; I water my couch with my tears.*

Luke 18:1 *And he spake a parable unto them to this end, that men ought always to pray, and not to faint;*

2 Saying, There was in a city a judge, which feared not God, neither regarded man:

3 And there was a widow in that city; and she came unto him, saying, Avenge me of mine adversary.

4 And he would not for a while: but afterward he said

within himself, Though I fear not God, nor regard man;
5 Yet because this widow troubleth me, I will avenge her, lest by her continual coming she weary me.
6 And the Lord said, Hear what the unjust judge saith.
7 And shall not God avenge his own elect, which cry day and night unto him, though he bear long with them?
8 I tell you that he will avenge them speedily. Nevertheless when the Son of man cometh, shall he find faith on the earth?

Scripture Discussion

In earlier chapters, it was pointed out that one's attitude toward prayer is very important. Attitude refers not only to what is being said, but it speaks of the mental posture of the person who is saying it. Throughout the word of God, people of God are seen praying with various physical postures. Each of these postures symbolizes a definite mental attitude toward God. Each teaches a different lesson about prayer.

Bowing the Knee. "Bowing the knee" is a posture that is seen throughout Scripture. Bowing the knee symbolizes total submission of an individual to God. The expression "bowing the knee" suggests that we have surrendered ourselves. Surrender comes, first of all, from the idea that we have taken away the thought of straying from God. When one is on one's knees, one doesn't really think of walking away from God. There is no thought of resistance or rebellion.

The Apostle Paul, in Ephesians 3, talks about bowing one's knees before God. Jesus Himself frequently took this posture before His Father. He took this posture in the Garden of Gethsemane (Luke 22:41).

Lifting Holy Hands. One of the other postures mentioned in the Word of God is "lifting holy hands." This posture symbolizes openness before the Lord and a willingness to abandon anything that would be insincere or that would demonstrate a lack of a proper attitude. The Apostle Paul, in 1 Timothy 2:8 says we should lift up holy hands.

In military terminology, when an enemy surrenders, the first thing he does is to raise his hands. The idea of complete and total surrender is involved in prayer also. The Apostle Paul speaks of this as he writes to Timothy, his son in the faith—the one he is instructing concerning proper conduct in the ministry. Paul says that praying is synonymous with lifting up holy hands. It is surrender that is involved in the idea of lifting of hands. Cleanliness or openness before God is suggested in the idea of the holy hands.

Stretching Out to God. Another posture that is associated with prayer is the idea of stretching out. Psalm 68:31 presents a picture of one who is stretching out to God. The hands are stretched out in this posture of prayer. The outstretched hands are an invitation to someone that we might embrace him or her. We do this sometimes when we want little children to come to us so that we can embrace them. We stretch out our hands to them.

We also stretch out our hands when we desire to appropriate something that is available to us. We reach for the object of our desire. In the case of prayer, though, we reach out to the One who can give us what we need.

We have looked at three physical postures that symbolize definite attitudes toward God and toward prayer: bowing the knee, lifting up holy hands, and stretching out our hands to God. Now let's look at a fourth physical posture: prostrating ourselves before God.

Prostrating Ourselves Before God. One of the first times the idea of prostrating oneself before God occurs in Scripture is in the life of Joshua. Joshua prostrated himself before the Lord and requested to know why the Lord had disappointed him in battle. He had come to fight the enemy and they had been chased just as bees, so to speak. Here we find that when one is prostrating, he is at the mercy of the one before whom he is prostrate. The idea conveyed is that we are at the mercy of God.

Tears. Yet a fifth physical expression of surrendering to God is found in Psalm 6:6. The tears of the Psalmist indicate complete brokenness before God. The idea of surrender, abandonment and a brokenness of heart is certainly involved here.

The five postures discussed above teach basic elements regarding prayer. A search through the Scriptures would reveal many others. May God richly bless us as we continue to learn about prayer and about communicating with God.

Case Studies in Prayer

Instructions: The following exercises will lead you into an in-depth study of the prayer of a weeping, sinful woman who washed the feet of Jesus with her tears. Each of the first four exercises consists of a series of "discovery" questions, followed by a summary question. The fifth exercise asks for a summary and an application. The sixth exercise asks you to apply the wisdom you gained from this "case study in prayer" to your private prayer life.

Prayer of a Weeping Woman

> And one of the Pharisees desired him that he would eat with him. And he went into the Pharisee's house, and sat down to meat. And, behold, a woman in the city, which was a sinner, when she knew that Jesus sat at meat in the Pharisee's house, brought an alabaster box of ointment,

And stood at his feet behind him weeping, and began to wash his feet with tears, and did wipe them with the hairs of her head, and kissed his feet, and anointed them with the ointment. Now when the Pharisee which had bidden him saw it, he spake within himself, saying, This man, if he were a prophet, would have known who and what manner of woman this is that toucheth him: for she is a sinner.

And Jesus answering said unto him...Seest thou this woman?

I entered into thine house, thou gavest me no water for my feet: but she hath washed my feet with tears, and wiped them with the hairs of her head. Thou gavest me no kiss: but this woman since the time I came in hath not ceased to kiss my feet. My head with oil thou didst not anoint: but this woman hath anointed my feet with ointment....

And he said unto her, Thy sins are forgiven...Thy faith hath saved thee; go in peace. (Luke 7:36-40, 44-46, 48, 50)

1. The Weeping Woman

The weeping woman came to Christ in tears.

a. Where did the weeping woman make contact with Jesus? (Luke 7:36-37)

b. What did she bring with her? (7:37)

c. Where did she stand in relation to Jesus? (7:38)

d. What did she do to Jesus' feet? (7:38)

e. How did the Pharisee react to the woman? (7:39)

f. How was the Pharisee's behavior toward Jesus

different from that of the weeping woman? (7:44-47)

g. Summary Question: Tell the basic facts in the story of the weeping woman's encounter with Jesus, as revealed in your answers to questions a-f. If you could translate her tears into words, what would her prayer sound like?

2. The Question of Sin

Most women who were called "sinners" were guilty of one of several sexual sins.

a. What is one type of sin of which this woman could have been guilty? (Numbers 5:11-31; Leviticus 20:10)

b. What is another type of sin of which this woman might have been guilty? (Luke 15:30; 1 Corinthians 6:15, 16; Hebrews 11:31)

c. What is yet another type of sin of which the woman might have been guilty? (Leviticus 19:29; 21:9; Proverbs 7:1-23)

d. How did religious leaders such as Pharisees treat people who were seen as beneath them in some way? (Luke 15:21; 18:11-12)

e. How were "harlots" usually treated under the Mosaic Law? (Genesis 38:24-25; Leviticus 21:9)

f. Summary Question: Review your answers to questions a-e. Then describe the problems that may have been facing this weeping, sinful woman. Then discuss her gestures toward Christ in the light of this information.

3. Jesus' Feet

Due to the heat and sand in New Testament Palestine, usually feet became dirty and uncomfortable very quickly.

a. What did the woman do to Jesus' feet? (Luke 7:38)

b. When a person fell at another's feet in New Testament Jewish culture, what did that person seek to communicate? (1 Samuel 25:23-24; 2 Kings 4:36-37; Esther 8:3; Mark 5:21-23)

c. When a person kissed someone's feet, what was being communicated? (Isaiah 49:22-3; 1 Kings 19:18)

d. Just being at the feet of another communicated what? (Judges 4:10; Acts 22:3)

e. Summary Question: If you could translate into words, the acts of kneeling at, washing and putting perfume on Jesus' feet, what would the prayer from this weeping woman to Jesus sound like?

4. Kissing

Kissing was another gesture of respect.

a. In New Testament Jewish culture, what was one thing that kissing symbolized? (Romans 16:16; 1 Corinthians 16:20; 2 Corinthians 13:12)

b. What was another thing that kissing might symbolize? (1 Peter 5:14)

c. What was yet another thing that kissing might symbolize? (Genesis 29:11)

d. Summary Question: If you could translate the one gesture of kissing Jesus into a prayer, what would the prayer from the weeping woman to Jesus sound like?

5. Summary Exercise: Review your answers to exercises #1-4 above. Then translate all of the physical gestures of the sinful, weeping woman toward Jesus into a written prayer.

6. Application: Review the various prayer postures which Dr. Banks discusses earlier in this chapter. Then review the postures of the weeping, sinful woman in the above Scripture passage. Experiment with various postures during your prayer time. Select postures which somehow express the basic core emotions that you are experiencing, or postures that communicate respect to the one to whom you are praying. Expect that your communication with God should be greatly improved.

CHAPTER SIX

Counting Costs and Benefits

There are many benefits that can be gained through prayer but there are no costs.

from Scripture
Jude 20 *But ye, beloved, building up yourselves on the most holy faith, praying in the Holy Ghost,*
21 Keep yourselves in the love of God, looking for the mercy of our Lord Jesus Christ unto eternal life.
Psalm 16:11 *Thou wilt show me the path of life: in thy presence is fulness of joy; at thy right hand there are pleasures for evermore.*
Philippians 4:6 *Be careful for nothing; but in every thing by prayer and supplication with thanksgiving let your requests be made known unto God.*
7 And the peace of God, which passeth all understanding, shall keep your hearts and minds through Christ Jesus.
Matthew 11:28 *Come unto me, all ye that labour and are heavy laden, and I will give you rest.*
29 Take my yoke upon you, and learn of me; for I am meek and lowly in heart: and ye shall find rest unto your souls.
30 For my yoke is easy, and my burden is light.
Hebrews 4:9 *There remaineth therefore a rest to the people of God.*

Scripture Discussion

A person from Mountainview Methodist Church in Beetle, Montana made a humorous comment many years ago. It went like this:

> No increase in the cost of prayer! Uncle Sam has increased the rates of postage, and it will cost more to write to friends, send communications and do business. However, God has made no increase in the cost of communication with heaven.
>
> Prepare your communication with sincerity, address it with care, seal it with faith and I am sure it will be properly delivered.

We've touched upon some of the truths this comment covers. We have dealt with preparing your communication with sincerity. We've dealt with that at length in relation to Ephesians 6:18. Moreover, the Epistle of Jude has given us insight into prayer.

Of particular interest is the phrase "praying in the Holy Ghost" found in Jude the 20th verse. This is what is meant by preparing your message with sincerity. It has to do with being sensitive to the fact that we're in the Holy Spirit.

The passage in Jude says to seal prayer with faith. Of course, without faith it is impossible to please God. Without faith it is impossible to approach God. For he who comes to God must believe that God exists and that He is a rewarder of those who diligently seek Him.

The Cost of Prayer. Everything has increased in cost today. Cost has increased in everything with which we deal, including communications and technology. But there's no increase in the cost of prayer.

With that thought in mind, we can be encouraged to pray and to be very sure in our own mind and heart that we have the right approach as it is suggested here.

Benefit #1: Fullness of Joy. We will recall that one reason Torrey says that prayer is important is that prayer in the name of Jesus Christ is the way Jesus appointed that His disciples might have fullness of joy (John 16:23, 24). In part, the joy is there because we get what we ask. But that is not the only reason. When we ask something definite of God and He gives it, how real God becomes! He is right there.

We find that we must and indeed need to be filled with the Spirit. The expression, "full of the Spirit" has to do with being able to sense God's companionship with us and to follow His guidance in all things. Of course, we need to enter into that communion with Him. We need to enter into that fellowship with Him. This is our privilege and our prerogative because He indwells us.

Of course, through prayer and through giving attention to the things that are pointed out in Ephesians 6:17, we prepare ourselves for fullness of joy. We find that God has encouraged us and the Lord Jesus Christ has assured us that it is through the Holy Spirit that we will be taught.

We will have things concerning Christ exposed to us—opened up to us and made intelligible to us. It is through the Holy Spirit of Christ that we have the energy to do the things our Lord says in Acts 1:8—"but ye shall receive power, after that the Holy Ghost has come upon you."

Through consistent and concerted prayer, we have available to us the fullness of the Spirit of God.

Benefit #2: Freedom from Anxiety. Torrey gives another reason that we ought to pray. Prayer for every care and anxiety of life with thanksgiving is the means that God has appointed for us to obtain freedom from all anxiety and the peace of God which passes all understanding.

The Apostle Paul, in Philippians 4:6, 7 points this out. He says that in everything, by prayer and supplication with thanksgiving, let our requests be made known unto God. He says *everything,* not some things. He doesn't say sometimes, but at *all* times. What will be the results? The peace of God will flood your hearts and minds! This is certainly the way that God has appointed that we attain freedom from anxiety.

Now the problems may remain. The difficulties may still be there. They are there as a discipline that God would have us go through in order to become, in fact, what He would have us become. But then the anxiety that goes with difficulties will not be there. In spite of all of those upsetting circumstances, we will have rest in Him because of our understanding.

Many times we hurry and crowd prayer out of our lives. We feel that we don't have time to pray. We believe there are other things that are more important than prayer. So we probably become exhausted and very weary at the close of the day. Then we just utter a very hasty phrase to the Lord. *But the time spent in prayer is not wasted. It is time invested. Big dividends accrue from that.*

God has designed that, through prayer, in the midst of anxieties and frustrations of life we experience rest. The Lord Jesus said, in Matthew 11:29, "Take my yoke upon you, and learn of me; for I am meek and lowly in heart: and ye shall find rest unto your souls." There remains a rest for the people of God. That rest, of course, is a faith resting in the Lord Jesus Christ.

Benefit #3: Preparation for the Day of Christ! Mr. Torrey suggests prayer is important because it is the means that Christ has appointed whereby our hearts will not experience Christ's Second Coming as a sudden snare.

We are admonished by the Apostle Paul as he writes to Titus, that we should be watching for the coming of the Lord. We are reminded of this in 1 Thessalonians 4, for the rapture is in view. Through prayer, we settle ourselves—our hearts and our minds. We anticipate the coming of the Lord Jesus Christ.

It is almost certain that, as a logical consequence of prayer, we commune with God. Then the anticipation of His coming is going to be heightened, deepened, and intensified. If we do not have that fellowship and communion with Him while we're here now, engaged in the battles of life, engaged in the growth process, engaged in the reaching out to those around us, then we're not going to be ready to welcome Him as He comes. His presence will not be a joy to us.

Torrey has pointed out that prayer is the means Christ has appointed that our hearts might not be overcharged with surfeiting and drunkenness with the cares of life. As a result, the day of Christ's coming overtakes us (Luke 21:34).

Finally, we end with yet another example from Torrey's book on prayer. It is entitled "The Two Prayers":

> Last night my little boy confessed to me some childish wrong. In kneeling at my knee, he prayed with tears, "Dear God, Make me a man like Daddy, wise and strong. I know you can."
>
> Then while he slept I knelt beside his bed and confessed my sins and prayed with low bowed head, "Oh, God, make me a child like my child here. Pure, guiltless, trusting thee with faith sincere."[1]

May we continue to become enriched in our prayers through faith!

1. Torrey, R.A., *The Power of Prayer and the Prayer of Power* (Grand Rapids: Zondervan Publishing House, 1955).

Case Studies in Prayer

Instructions: The following exercises will lead you into an in-depth study of a prayer of Stephen, the martyr. Each of the first four exercises consists of a series of "discovery" questions, followed by a summary question. The fifth exercise asks for a summary and an application.

The sixth exercise asks you to apply the wisdom you gained from this "case study in prayer" to your private prayer life.

Stephen's Prayer

And Stephen, full of faith and power, did great wonders and miracles among the people. Then there arose certain of the synagogue, which is called the synagogue of the Libertines, and Cyrenians, and Alexandrians, and of them of Cilicia and of Asia, disputing with Stephen.

But he, being full of the Holy Ghost, looked up steadfastly into heaven, and saw the glory of God, and Jesus standing on the right hand of God. And said, Behold, I see heavens opened, and the Son of man standing on the right hand of God.

Then they cried out with a loud voice, and stopped their ears, and ran upon him with one accord. And cast him out of the city, and stoned him: and the witnesses laid down their clothes at a young man's feet, whose name was Saul.

And they stoned Stephen, calling upon God, and saying, Lord Jesus receive my spirit. And he kneeled down, and cried with a loud voice, Lord, lay not this sin to their charge. And when he had said this, he fell asleep. (Acts 6:8, 9; 7:55-60)

1. Stephen's Position in the Church

Stephen had gained much wisdom in his spiritual life. This wisdom is reflected in his prayer.

a. What was Stephen's job in the New Testament Church? (Acts 6:1-6)

b. For what was Stephen known? (6:5, 8)

c. What was one of Stephen's greatest gifts? (6:10)

d. Summary Question: Considering your answers to questions a-c, what are ways that Stephen's background may have prepared him for the moment when he was martyred?

2. Stephen's Enemies

Stephen's enemies were from areas where the Gospel of Jesus Christ was spreading very rapidly.

a. How many different groups of people conspired together to bring about Stephen's death? (Acts 6:9)

b. Present some facts about Cyrene, the home of some of those who were conspiring against Stephen. (Acts 2:1-4, 10; 11:18-20; 13:1-3; Matthew 27:32; Mark 15:18-21)

c. Present some facts about Alexandria, the home of another group that was conspiring against Stephen. (Acts 18:24-28)

d. Present some facts about Cilicia, the home of yet another group that was conspiring against Stephen. (Acts 15:40-41; Acts 21:39-40; Galatians 1:11-24)

e. Present some facts about Asia, the home of yet another group that was conspiring against Stephen. (Acts 2:1-4, 9; 19:8-22; 20:3-4, 16, 18; 1

Corinthians 16:19; 2 Timothy 1:15; 1 Peter 1:1)

f. Summary Question: The people who conspired against Stephen were from communities where Christian communities were growing. What might this fact have had to do with their hostility against Stephen?

3. Stephen's Death Compared to Jesus Christ's Crucifixion

Stephen's life and death is an example of how our Lord's disciples would "drink from the bitter cup" in the same way that Jesus did.

a. What is one way in which Stephen and Jesus Christ were very similar? (Acts 6:8; Matthew 9:27-31, 32-33; Mark 7:31-37)

b. Compare and contrast the concerns of representatives of synagogues conspiring against Stephen with the concerns of those who conspired against Christ. (Acts 6:10, 12; Matthew 26:57-66; 27:1, 11-14; Mark 14:55-65; 15:1-15)

c. In what ways is Stephen's prayer (Acts 7:59-60) similar to our Lord's prayer on Calvary? (Matthew 28:50; Mark 15:37; Luke 23:34, 46; John 19:30)

d. Summary Question: Summarize the similarities and differences between Stephen and our Lord Jesus Christ.

4. Stephen's Trial

Stephen prayed in the midst of a very difficult situation, yet he achieved peace in the midst of it.

a. What role in society did the religious leaders who put Stephen on trial have? (Matthew 5:22; 26:59; Mark 14:55; 15:1; Luke 22:2; John 11:47; Acts 4:1, 13-15)

b. What were some of the types of people who made up this council of religious leaders? (Acts 5:17, 34; John 18:22; Mark 14:63-65)

c. What was the nature of the charge against Stephen? (Acts 6:11; Romans 2:24; Luke 5:21; Matthew 26:65; John 10:36)

d. What was the usual punishment for blasphemy? (Leviticus 24:11-16)

e. Stephen told the religious leaders that they had what in common with their ancestors? (Acts 7:9, 26-27, 37-41, 51-53)

f. Summary Question: Considering your answers to questions a-e, why did Stephen's reference to Jesus Christ in his prayer (7:56) cause such a violent response in the religious leaders? (7:54, 57)

5. Summary Exercise: Dr. Banks mentions the importance of praying in the Holy Ghost for: fullness of joy, freedom from anxiety, fullness of the spirit and preparation for the coming of Christ. In what ways is Stephen's prayer an example of all of this?

6. Application: Christians sometimes find themselves in the midst of very painful experiences. These occur at our places of employment, in our homes and sometimes within the church itself. The next time you are in a painful or stressful experience, and you feel under attack by Satan, find a quiet spot, acknowledge the presence of the Holy Spirit, and cry out to the Lord.

CHAPTER SEVEN

Praying Regularly

The Bible contains many examples of great men of God who prayed regularly.

from Scripture
John 17:1 *These words spake Jesus, and lifted up his
eyes to heaven, and said, Father, the hour is come; glorify
thy Son, that thy Son also may glorify thee:*
*2 As thou hast given him power over all flesh, that he
should give eternal life to as many as thou hast given
him.*
*3 And this is life eternal, that they might know thee
the only true God, and Jesus Christ, whom thou hast
sent.*
*4 I have glorified thee on the earth: I have finished
the work which thou gavest me to do.*
*5 And now, O Father, glorify thou me with thine own
self with the glory which I had with thee before the world
was.*
Psalm 5:3 *My voice shalt thou hear in the morning, O
Lord; in the morning will I direct my prayer unto thee,
and will look up.*
Psalm 88:1 *O Lord God of my salvation, I have cried
day and night before thee:*
*2 Let my prayer come before thee: incline thine ear
unto my cry;*
*3 For my soul is full of troubles: and my life draweth
nigh unto the grave.*
Psalm 55:17 *Evening, and morning, and at noon, will I
pray, and cry aloud: and he shall hear my voice.*
Luke 6:12 *And it came to pass in those days, that he*

went out into a mountain to pray, and continued all night in prayer to God.

Scripture Discussion

The Book of Psalm is a good place to research for insights into prayer. The psalmist mentions five schedules that are good for prayer.

Prayer in the Morning. In the psalms we find suggested over and over again the idea of praying in the morning. There are good reasons for praying in the morning. First of all, we are fresh. We have not become distracted with the issues of the day. Therefore it is a good time to deal with the matters of trusting God. It is a good time to preface our day's activities with prayer so that the rest of the day will flow easily along.

The Lord Jesus Christ was known to go out early in the morning and continue in prayer.

Prayer Twice a Day. In some places in Scripture, it is recommended that we pray twice daily. In Psalm 88 we find the psalmist saying that he cries day and night before the Lord. Here we have a recommendation to pray, not only in the morning, but both day and night. There must have been regularity in the psalmist's praying. He was not sporadic. He had a definite time set apart.

Prayer Three Times a Day. In some portions of the Old Testament, we find the recommendation to pray three times each day. In Daniel 6:10 we find Daniel doing this. Daniel did this at a time when he was reprimanded for having prayed to God and for having discounted the contract that was made between the King and those who would pray to God.

Daniel did not begin praying when the crisis came. His preparation for prayer was always in the heart. We should follow this example. Then prayer does not become something that we enter into with a feeling of strangeness. Daniel had been praying in his heart. Then when the decree was signed that no one should pray to any other God, he simply continues praying. It was already his habit or practice.

In Psalm 55:17, the psalmist David says that he also prays in the morning, at noon and in the evening. In Luke 6:12, we find our Lord Jesus Christ Himself praying at various times during the day. Our Lord Jesus Christ gives us an example of liberty and sustained praying. He recommended praying out of the heart and out of the depths of the heart for our and others' needs.

No doubt when Christ was confronted with various experiences such as healing the sick, raising the dead, teaching the disciples, and casting out demons during the day, our Lord Jesus Christ then had to prepare for a time of communion with God.

It had to be a time in which He, the God-Man both interceded as Man on earth, and shared as God with an equal, regarding the things that He did and the things that He accomplished during the day.

When the Lord came to the end of His life as recorded in John 17, He really prayed a high priestly prayer. In the first five verses, He affirmed the fact that He had done what God had laid upon His hands and heart to do. So much of our prayer time is taken up with our accomplished tasks, or our requests for a supply of some need to accomplish a task that has been assigned to us.

Having several times during the day that we set apart for prayer is one way of praying without ceasing. Of course, by way of review, praying without ceasing is recommended by the Apostle Paul in 1 Thessalonians 5:17. There he says that he marvels as he looks at the depth of spiritual insight that the Thessalonians had with just a little involvement with the Apostle Paul's teaching and preaching.

Paul was in Thessalonia less than a month. After he

left there, the Spirit gave insights in how to grow and increase spiritually as a result of what he had told them. As a result, he told them that he prayed for them without ceasing. Of course, in order to do that, there had to be preparation of heart and mind.

All Night Prayer. There are also psalms which suggest praying all night. An example is when David says, "All night long I water my bed with tears."

However, whatever the prayer pattern we establish for ourselves, it is important to prepare for prayer. There are many acts that can serve as good preparation for prayer: adoration, confession, thanksgiving, supplication and surrender. These particular words frame the gamut of our prayers, whether the prayers are private, public or spontaneous. These words come to us from our Lord Jesus Christ.

Confession. First there is confession. We need to be sure that, as we pray, the channel of communication is open. That channel, of course, is closed and restricted if there is sin in our lives. The Bible tells us that if we regard iniquity in our hearts the Lord will not hear us. We need the type of confession that is stated in 1 John 1:9: "If we confess our sins, he is faithful and just to forgive us our sins and to cleanse us from all unrighteousness."

Thanksgiving. There should also be an element of thanksgiving in all that we do—whether it is our service, whether it is our praise, or whether it is our prayer.

Supplication. Then there is supplication. We ought to beseech God regarding some particular aspect of our lives or regarding one of our needs.

Intercession. Then there ought to be intercession. We should pray for others.

Surrender. Finally, there should be surrender. We need that as we approach the throne of Grace. "For he that cometh to God must believe that he is, and that he is a rewarder of them that diligently seek him" (Hebrews 11:6).

Of course, the Bible also suggests that we pray without ceasing. May God bless our meditation upon these words!

Case Studies in Prayer

Instructions: The following exercises will lead you into an in-depth study of the corporate or public prayer life of Daniel. Each of the first four exercises consists of a series of "discovery" questions, followed by a summary question. The fifth exercise asks for a summary and an application.

The sixth exercise asks you to apply the wisdom you gained from this "case study in prayer" to your private prayer life.

Daniel's Prayer Times

> Now when Daniel knew that the writing was signed, he went into his house; and his windows being open in his chamber toward Jerusalem, he kneeled upon his knees three times a day, and prayed, and gave thanks before his God, as he did aforetime.
>
> Then these men assembled, and found Daniel praying and making supplication before his God. (Daniel 6:10-11)

1. Daniel's Background

   Daniel's unique history had an influence on the seriousness with which he regarded prayer.

   a. Daniel lived at a time when what had happened to Jerusalem? (Daniel 1:1)

b. To what group of people did Daniel originally belong? (1:3-6)
c. How did Daniel come to live at the royal court? (1:3-6)
d. What was outstanding about Daniel? (1:4, 17, 19-20)
e. From the very beginning, how did Daniel deal with the "system"? (1:8-16)
f. Eventually, what became Daniel's role in Babylon, under Nebuchadnezzar? (2:48)
g. Summary Question: Considering your answers to questions a-f, describe the aspects of Daniel's personality and history that would cause him to have the stubbornness to obey God rather than man?

2. Daniel's Career

Daniel saw the Lord act miraculously in his career.

a. What initially caused Daniel to become ruler over the "whole province of Babylon" under Nebuchadnezzar? (2:14; 2:1-4, 10-18, 16, 19-20, 25-26, 28, 46-48; 4)
b. What caused Daniel to be elevated to "third ruler of the kingdom" under Belteshazzar? (5:10-28, 29)
c. What happened to Daniel's career under Darius, Belteshazzar's successor? (5:30—6:3)
d. What did Daniel experience under King Belteshazzar? (7:1-15; 8:1, 27)
e. Summary Question: Explain how Daniel's experiences under the various kings might have prepared him to take a stand for the Lord in the face of uncertainty.

3. Daniel's Persecution and Deliverance

   Daniel's experiences with persecution and deliverance had a definite influence on his character.

   a. How did many people come to view Daniel's successes? (6:4-5)
   b. How did Daniel's enemies go about "entrapping" him? (6:6-13)
   c. In the short run, was their plot successful? (6:14-17)
   d. In the long run, was the plot of Daniel's enemies successful? Explain. (6:18-28)
   e. Summary Question: There seemed to be an "unseen power" operating behind the scenes in Daniel's life. Describe how Daniel's regularity in prayer may have helped to unleash this "unseen power."

4. Tradition and Daniel's Prayer Life

   Daniel must have grown up reading about the Patriarchs in whose lives prayer played an important role.

   a. What role might Abraham's example have played in the shaping of Daniel's prayer life? (Genesis 18:22-27; 20:17)
   b. What role might Isaac's prayer life have played in the shaping of Daniel's prayer life? (25:21)
   c. How might Jacob's prayer life have played a role in the shaping of Daniel's prayer life? (32:9-12, 24-30)
   d. How might Moses' prayer life have influenced the development of Daniel's prayer life? (Exodus 17:4-6; 19:3-6; 20)
   e. How might knowledge of Hannah's prayers have influenced the development of Daniel's prayer life? (1 Samuel 1:5-20)

f. Summary Question: What role might the Old Testament Scriptures have played in Daniel's respect for the power of prayer?

5. Summary Exercise: Dr. Banks recommended that we establish a daily prayer schedule in order to have regularity in our communications with God. Review your answers to exercises 1 - 4. Then describe the impact that this regularity in prayer had in Daniel's life.

6. Application: Give some careful thought to your daily routine. Then determine times and places where you can meet with God on a regular basis.

CHAPTER EIGHT

Praying for Outcome

Through prayer we can accomplish spiritual growth, power to work, evangelism, blessings to the church, and communication with God.

from Scripture

Psalm 139:23 *Search me, O God, and know my heart: try me, and know my thoughts:*
24 And see if there be any wicked way in me, and lead me in the way everlasting.

2 Corinthians 3:18 *But we all, with open face beholding as in a glass the glory of the Lord, are changed into the same image from glory to glory, even as by the Spirit of the Lord.*

Acts 1:8 *But ye shall receive power, after that the Holy Ghost is come upon you: and ye shall be witnesses unto me both in Jerusalem, and in all Judaea, and in Samaria, and unto the uttermost part of the earth.*

2 Corinthians 9:11 *Being enriched in every thing to all bountifulness, which causeth through us thanksgiving to God.*
12 For the administration of this service not only supplieth the want of the saints, but is abundant also by many thanksgivings unto God;
13 Whiles by the experiment of this ministration they glorify God for your professed subjection unto the gospel of Christ, and for your liberal distribution unto them, and unto all men;
14 And by their prayer for you, which long after you for the exceeding grace of God in you.
15 Thanks be unto God for his unspeakable gift.

Scripture Discussion

By way of review, we have been presenting some of the reasons that Torrey, in his book, *Teach Us to Pray* stated that prayer is important. One of the reasons Torrey says prayer is important is that we accomplish things through prayer. There are four things that Torrey says are secured through prayer. These are: spiritual growth, power to work, evangelism, blessings to the church, and communication with God.

Prayer and Spiritual Growth. First of all, prayer promotes spiritual growth as almost nothing else—indeed as nothing else but prayer and Bible study. They go hand in hand. We need to grow spiritually. The Apostle Peter admonishes us to grow in grace, and in the knowledge of our Lord and Saviour Jesus Christ. This growth in grace is very much connected to the life of prayer.

The Two Go Together. Bible study and prayer. It is through prayer that sin in our lives is brought to light. The hint of those things of darkness is revealed to us. The Psalmist David prayed to this end in Psalm 139. He was saying, "Develop me. Help me to grow in the way everlasting!"

As we pray, inequity is made known to us. Then, as we meet God in prayer, we gaze into His face, and as Paul tells us in 2 Corinthians 3:18 we are changed into God's same image. We certainly need to be changed into His image.

Prayer and Power. We get power or energy through prayer. In Acts 1:8 we are told that we will receive power after the Holy Ghost is come upon us. Therefore, we realize the fullness of the Spirit of God as this spirit is released.

Then we notice that prayer brings power into our work. We need to sense a surge of energy as we do the work of the Lord. So often we're tired and seemingly dissipated as we look at the matter of the work of the Lord. Even in prayer, we sometimes experience drowsiness or a loss of energy (particularly as we approach the matter of confronting the enemy and the powers of darkness).

However, the energy for this particular work is given to us as we pray. If we wish power for any work for which God calls us, whether it's preaching or teaching or personal work, or whether it is the ordinary routines of life such as rearing our children, or relating to our husband or wife, we can get that power through earnest prayer. We need to keep this fact in mind.

Prayer and Evangelism. Prayer leads to the conversion of others. As we read in Ephesians 6:18 we should pray always. Through prayer, we avail for others. Prevailing for others, those that are the servants of God, and those that are the saints of God. Then Paul says that God sends utterance to us so that we may open our mouths boldly and make known the mystery of the Gospel. As we search for and properly sensitize ourselves to the Word of God and the Spirit of God, that we become able to speak to others in a saving way. This is a direct result of prayer.

Prayer and Blessings of the Church. Prayer brings blessings to the church. Paul spoke of the Philippian church giving to his ministry and being blessed as a result of the fact that they contributed to him. We find that in 2 Corinthians 9.

In dealing with the matter of giving, in 2 Corinthians 9:11 Paul connects the matter of praying with blessing and enrichment of the Church. He talks about the church's giving being a benefit to the church. We also see here the matter of their praying—their being a blessing to the church.

The devil hates us as individuals and he hates us as a group, the Church. He seeks to defeat the church at every turn. As we look at the church today, in its local setting, we find that the church is splintered by divisiveness: false doctrine, and various corruptions of life. However, God has said that through prayer these things that divide the church can be corrected.

Entering into prayer as he has told us will certainly correct many of these things. Torrey says prayer will root out heresy, allay misunderstandings, keep away jealousy and animosities, obliterate immoralities, and bring in the full tide of God's reviving grace. History abundantly proves this.

In the case of the church locally and universally, it may be the hour of darkest portent. However, for those believing men and women who met together and cried to God, their answer has come. How rewarding, how refreshing and oh, how satisfying.

Prayer and Communication with God. Prayer is communication with God. Prayer brings us into fellowship with Him. Prayer brings us into a sense of belonging to God. As a child we need to sense that belonging. As God's children, we have a feeling of deep dependency. We know that we are nothing in ourselves. We're not able in ourselves to do anything. But He is our sufficiency.

May we become men and women of prayer!

Case Studies in Prayer

Instructions: The following exercises will lead you into an in-depth study of the role of prayer in the early church. Each of the first five exercises consists of a series of "discovery" questions, followed by a summary question. The sixth exercise asks for a summary and an application.

The seventh exercise asks you to apply the wisdom you gained from this "case study in prayer" to your private prayer life.

Prayer in the New Testament Church

> And they continued stedfastly in the apostles' doctrine and fellowship, and in breaking of bread, and in prayers. And fear came upon every soul: and many wonders and signs were done by the apostles. And all that believed were together, and had all things common; And sold their possessions and goods, and parted them to all men, as every man had need.
>
> And they, continuing daily with one accord in the temple, and breaking bread from house to house, did eat their meat with gladness and singleness of heart, Praising God and having favour with all the people. And the Lord added to the church daily such as should be saved. (Acts 2:42-47)

1. The Early Church

The daily lives of members of the early church must have formed the content of many of their private and group prayers.

a. Who were some of the people of the New Testament Church? (Matthew 28:16-20; Acts 1:12-14, 23-26; 2:1-21, 38-41)

b. Form a mission statement (statement of purpose) of the early church. (Matthew 28:20; Acts 2:42-47; 1 Corinthians 12:4-12; 16:1-4; Romans 15:25-28; 2 Corinthians 8:1-7)

c. What was a common enemy of all members of the church? (Acts 4:1-3; 6:9-13; 8:1, 14-20; 9:20-24; 12:1-5; 14:1-7)

d. What was the main source of power for the early church? (Acts 1:8; 2:1-21)

e. Considering your answers to questions a-d, list

items that might have formed the content of some of the group and private prayers in the early church. (Acts 2:42)

2. Prayer and Christian Education in the Early Church (Acts 2:42)

   There seemed to be a direct relationship between prayer and learning in the early church.

   a. What doctrine did the apostles teach members of the church? (Acts 2:14-41)
   b. Was studying and teaching a low priority in the early church? Explain. (Isaiah 54:13; 2 Timothy 2:15; 3:14-15; Acts 2:42; 13:1; 2 Thessalonians 2:15; Ephesians 4:11; James 2:1; 3:1)
   c. What is the evidence that study prepared people for salvation? (John 6:45; Acts 2:41)
   d. What is the evidence that study was used as a preparation for prayer? (Acts 2:42)
   e. Summary Question: In the early church, what was the relationship between prayer, miracles, redistribution of wealth, social action programs, worship of God and evangelism? Explain.

3. Prayer and Spiritual Growth in the Early Church

   There seemed to be a direct relationship between prayer and spiritual growth in the early church.

   a. What impact did prayer have on the spiritual growth of the early church at Jerusalem? Explain. (Acts 1:14-16; 2:1-4, 41, 42)
   b. What impact did the Apostle Paul's prayers have on spiritual growth and faith of members of the church at Rome? (Romans 1:1-9)
   c. What impact did the Apostle Paul's prayers have on the church at Corinth? (1 Corinthians 1:1-7)

d. What impact did Paul's prayers have on the spiritual growth of the saints, bishops and deacons at Philippi? (Philippians 1:1-10)

e. What impact did the Apostle Paul's prayers have on the church at Colossae? (Colossians 1:1-16)

f. What impact did the Apostle Paul's prayers have on the church at Thessalonia? (1 Thessalonians 1:1-10)

g. What impact did the Apostle Paul's prayers have on his personal spiritual growth? (Acts 9:6, 17-20, 22)

h. Considering your answers to questions a-g, explain how the model of the early church's pattern of prayer and Bible study, and the model of the Apostle Paul's prayers must have spread throughout the Roman Empire, where Christian communities were being established.

4. Prayer and Power in the Early Church

There seemed to be a direct relationship between prayer and power in the early church.

a. What was the first dramatic demonstration of how prayer could lead to power in the early church? (Acts 1:8; 2:14-21, 1-4, 37-41)

b. What role did prayer play in the healing of the man at the temple gate? (Acts 3:1-10)

c. What role did prayer play in the healing of Dorcas? (Acts 9:36-42)

d. What role did prayer play in the release of Peter from prison? (Acts 12:1-18)

e. Summary Question: Dr. Banks, in his radio broadcasts, mentioned that Christians receive power through prayer. Consider your answers to questions a-d. Then re-examine Acts 2:42-47. Then present the evidence that there is a relationship between prayer and power.

5. Prayer and Evangelism

   There seemed to be a direct relationship between prayer and winning souls to Christ in the early church.

   a. What impact did prayer have on the winning of souls in the early church? (Acts 2:47, 1, 2, 38-41)
   b. What role did prayer play in the salvation of Sergius Paulus on the isle of Paphos? (Acts 13:6-12)
   c. What role did prayer play in the salvation of Gentiles at Antioch? (Acts 13:3-4, 14-16, 42-49)
   d. What role did prayer play in the salvation of souls in Macedonia? (Acts 13:3-4; 16:6-18)
   e. What role did prayer play in the saving of souls in prison? (Acts 16:16-40)
   f. Summary Question: Consider your answers to a-e above. Then re-examine Acts 2:42-47. Explain the role of prayer in the missionary outreach of the early church.

6. Summary Exercise: Dr. Banks, in his radio broadcasts, pointed out that prayer results in: spiritual growth, spiritual power, saving of souls, blessings to the church and improved communications with God. Explain how the early church and the prayer life of the Apostle Paul are examples of this.

7. Application: Reflect on your church's prison ministry, evangelism programs, social action programs, and Christian education programs. Then list ways that group prayer could become a more visible component of these activities and programs.

CHAPTER NINE

Praying While Ministering

Jesus healed many people. However, He prayed for them while He ministered to them.

from Scripture
Luke 5:12 *And it came to pass, when he was in a certain city, behold a man full of leprosy: who seeing Jesus fell on his face, and besought him, saying, Lord, if thou wilt, thou canst make me clean.*
13 And he put forth his hand, and touched him, saying, I will: be thou clean. And immediately the leprosy departed from him.
14 And he charged him to tell no man: but go, and show thyself to the priest, and offer for thy cleansing, according as Moses commanded, for a testimony unto them.
15 But so much the more went there a fame abroad of him: and great multitudes came together to hear, and to be healed by him of their infirmities.
16 And he withdrew himself into the wilderness, and prayed.
Mark 1:32 *And at even, when the sun did set, they brought unto him all that were diseased, and them that were possessed with devils.*
33 And all the city was gathered together at the door.
34 And he healed many that were sick of divers diseases, and cast out many devils; and suffered not the devils to speak, because they knew him.
35 And in the morning, rising up a great while before day, he went out, and departed into a solitary place, and there prayed.

Scripture Discussion

Being God as well as Man, it goes without saying that, on earth, Christ felt the necessity of praying as a human being would. We should really pay attention to this. Prayer was very important to our Lord. It was more important than teaching and healing.

Christ Withdrew Himself to Pray. One day a great multitude came out to be healed, but after a while, Jesus withdrew Himself into the desert in order to pray. Luke 5:12-16 is an example of this. In the midst of this great healing campaign, the Lord Jesus Christ withdrew Himself and prayed. However, most of us, if we had been enjoying the type of popularity that Jesus experienced, and had that kind of opportunity to share in the way He shared, would have stayed out in the city as long as the people came.

In contrast, the Lord Jesus Christ sensed the importance of prayer. It was essential to Him to have communion with the Father. In communing with the Father, He must have shared what was going on in His earthly ministry. What would be a more effective way to accomplish the ministry that He had been sent to accomplish?

It is certain that one of the things on the Lord Jesus Christ's mind was just a matter of fellowshiping with the Father—a matter of sharing with God while He was in the midst of His ministry. The Lord Jesus sought the kind of fellowship with God in prayer that we all need.

Christ Rose Before Dawn to Pray. Jesus rose up a great while before day and went out to a desert and prayed. The Lord Jesus Christ realized the importance of prayer and the significance of it. If the Lord realized the significance of this, then, as His disciples, we need to see the importance of it also.

We see here that Christ prayed early in the morning. Early, for any one of us, would be determined by our day's schedule or routine. If we are to be up and out by 7:00 a.m., early for us might be about 5:00 a.m. or 6:00 a.m. If someone has to get out earlier than that, early in the morning could mean as early as 4:00 a.m.

Whatever the situation, we see that the Lord Jesus Christ gave morning prayer top priority. He got together with God before the problems of the day came upon Him and before He would not have the natural energy to pray. Later in the day, He would not have the opportunity to just fellowship with the Father as He would want.

Let us also put morning prayer as a top priority. Someone said that it is better to pray in the morning because after the events and problems of the day face us, we are not as fresh. We are not as ready. We are not as alive and alert. We want to be at our best as we converse with God. It makes sense for us to do this early in the morning.

Christ Thought That Prayer Was the Best Thing That You Can Do for Someone. One thing we notice about the Lord Jesus is that sometimes, instead of aiding persons in the way they may need it, He prayed for them. Take Peter for example. When He was involved with Peter in Luke chapter 22, He said that Satan desired to have Peter so that Satan might sift Peter as wheat, to use a common vernacular.

Satan desired that he might shake Peter up. Christ said, instead, that He would pray for Peter. He would pray that Peter's faith would not fail. Here the Lord Jesus Christ could have performed the miracle of providing Peter with some miraculous aid along the way. But He said, in this case (Luke 22:32), that He would pray for him instead.

In other words, our Lord was saying, "I know that John needs prayer. I know that Philip needs prayer. I know that Bartholomew and the rest of the disciples need prayer. In fact, I know that there are people here in the city of Jerusalem who need prayer, but I will pray for you, Peter."

When we think of prayer, we need to realize that needs for prayer are very specific. From this, we see that the best thing we can do for anyone is to pray. When the Lord Jesus Christ said to Peter that He would pray for him, that should have heartened Peter. That should have strengthened Peter greatly. That should have alerted Peter to that which was before him. However, unfortunately, Peter did not feel the impact of that statement, just as many of us would not.

Christ Prayed for More Laborers. The Lord Jesus Christ, in another sense, highlighted the importance of prayer. In Matthew 9:36-37, He saw the multitudes of people and He was moved with compassion. At that time, He said to His disciples that surely the harvest was plenteous but the laborers were few. He said that they should pray that the Lord of the harvest would send more laborers. He knew that there was work to be done.

Today, there are few laborers. Most of us have tried to formulate some type of plan to get more people involved in the work that needs to be done. That is why the Lord says that we should pray to the Lord of the harvest. Why does He ask us to do this rather than do something else?

Well, the matter of sending forth workers for the work of the Lord is a work of the Holy Spirit. The Holy Spirit calls. He commissions. He challenges. He equips. He teaches. He empowers. He leads. He guides. As we pray to the Father, the Holy Spirit will then operate. He will take the opportunity of working in the hearts and minds of the people.

Christ Wants Us to Be Specific in Prayer. It is important to be specific when we pray. Pray for people as they request specific things. For example, if there is a young man or woman in your congregation with whom the Lord is working—a person who has a sincere desire to be in the Lord's ministry—we should pray pointedly for that person. This is what the Lord Jesus had in mind in Matthew 9:38 when He says, "Pray ye therefore the Lord of the harvest, that he will send forth laborers into his harvest."

This, again, highlights the importance of prayer.

Again, we can note that prayer is important to the Lord Jesus because that's what He's doing right now. Hebrews 7:25 says "he ever liveth to make intercession" for us. The idea of making intercession brings us face to face with the fact that the Lord Jesus Christ is always praying for us. As a result of His praying, we are strengthened. We are comforted. We are taught. We are encouraged, and we have our hope spurred on.

In Luke chapter 3, as the Lord Jesus is being baptized, He comes up out of the water and prays as He begins His public ministry. We find Him praying consistently throughout His life. In Luke 18:1, the Lord says "men ought always to pray, and not to faint." The last thing that the Lord Jesus Christ did on the cross was to pray.

Jesus' ministry began in prayer and His ministry continued with prayer. The strength He drew from His relationship with God is shown by the result of His life. Not only is the Lord Jesus praying for us now, prayer characterized His life on earth.

Case Studies in Prayer

Instructions: The following exercises will lead you into an in-depth study of Moses' intercessory prayer for the Children of Israel. Each of the first four exercises consists of a series of "discovery" questions, followed by a summary question. The fifth exercise asks for a summary and an application.

The sixth exercise asks you to apply the wisdom you gained from this "case study in prayer" to your private prayer life.

A Prayer for the Children of Israel

And the Lord said unto Moses, How long will this people provoke me? and how long will it be ere they believe me, for all the signs which I have shown among them? I will smite Them with the pestilence, and disinherit them, and will make thee a greater nation and mightier than they.

> And Moses said unto the Lord, Then the Egyptians shall hear it...and they will tell it to the inhabitants of this land: for they have heard that thou Lord art among this people, that thou Lord art seen face to face, and that thy cloud standeth over them, and that thou goest before them, by day time in a pillar of a cloud, and in a pillar of fire by night.
>
> Now if thou shalt kill all this people as one man, then the nations which have heard the fame of thee will speak, saying, Because the Lord was not able to bring this people into the land which he sware unto them, therefore he hath slain them in the wilderness. And now, I beseech thee, let the power of my Lord be great, according as thou hast spoken, saying,
>
> The Lord is longsuffering, and of great mercy, forgiving iniquity and transgression, and by no means clearing the guilty, visiting the iniquity of the fathers upon the children unto the third and fourth generation.
>
> Pardon, I beseech thee, the iniquity of

this people according unto the greatness of thy mercy, and as thou hast forgiven this people, from Egypt even until now.

And the Lord said, I have pardoned according to thy word: (Numbers 14:11-20)

1. Moses' Ministry among the Children of Israel

In Moses' prayer he reflects on the history, purpose and existence of the Children of Israel.

a. What is the ministry to which Moses was called? (Exodus 3:1-12)

b. What is one major event that had occurred in Moses' ministry by the time of his prayer in the Book of Numbers? (14:10-31)

c. What is another miracle that God had performed in the sight of the Children of Israel? (16:2-15)

d. What are some promises that God had made to the Children of Israel? (19:5-6)

e. What is one of the things that the Children of Israel did that angered God? (32:1-8)

f. What was God's response to the sins that the Children of Israel committed? (32:7-10; Numbers 14:10-12)

g. Summary Question: Considering your answers to questions a-f, what references to the history of the Children of Israel are reflected in Moses' prayer?

2. Moses' Prayer Life

Moses is an example of one who prayed while he ministered to people.

a. In what types of places did Moses go to commune with God? (Exodus 3:1-3; 19:20; Deuteronomy 34:1)

b. Did Moses limit the time he spent in prayer to a few minutes in the morning? (Exodus 24:18)

c. What is one type of direction that Moses needed to get from God for his people? (25:1-9)

d. What is another type of direction Moses needed to get for his people? (31:18; 34:27-28)

e. What is another type of direction Moses needed to get from God for his people? (Leviticus 8:1-9; 3:5-16)

f. What is yet another type of direction that Moses needed to get from God for his people? (Exodus 11:1-4)

g. What is one type of prayer that Moses offered for his people? (32:30; Numbers 11:1-3)

h. Summary Question: Considering your answers to questions a-g, what are the ways in which Moses prayed while in the midst of his ministry?

3. Intercessory Prayer

It has always been important for one human being to pray for another.

a. Why is it so important for Christ to be our Mediator? (1 John 2:1; Hebrews 4:14-16; 7:25; 13:15)

b. What role does the Holy Spirit play in mediation? (Romans 8:26-27)

c. What role do other human beings play in mediation? (1 Samuel 12:23; 1 Kings 18:36-39; Matthew 5:44; 1 Timothy 2:1)

d. Considering questions a-c, summarize the ways in which Christ, the Holy Spirit and other human beings can make intercession for us.

4. Other Prayers of Moses for His People

   Moses was a praying man. The Bible contains many different types of his prayers.

   a. Did all of Moses' prayers consist primarily of petitions? (Exodus 15) Explain.

   b. Did all of Moses' prayers consist primarily of seeking directions from the Lord? (Deuteronomy 26:7-8)

   c. What other types of prayers did Moses send forth to God? (31:30—32:3)

   d. Considering your answers to questions a-c, what are the various types of prayers that Moses sent forth to God as he ministered to the people?

5. Summary Exercise: Dr. Banks said that we should make prayer a very active part of our ministries. This would mean that we:

   a) withdraw periodically to pray.

   b) pray for those whom we serve.

   c) rise early and pray "at the top of the morning."

   d) pray for more laborers.

   e) be specific in prayer.

   How was Moses' prayer life an example of praying actively while ministering?

6. Application: Consider again, Moses' prayer life. Also review the suggestions made by Dr. Banks regarding praying while carrying out your ministries. Make a checklist and implement Dr. Banks' suggestions on a daily basis.

CHAPTER TEN

Praying for God's Servants

Many times we feel that if a person is strong in the faith we do not need to pray for him or her. However, Paul prayed for missionaries located throughout the Roman Empire.

from Scripture

Colossians 1:9 *For this cause we also, since the day we heard it, do not cease to pray for you, and to desire that ye might be filled with the knowledge of his will in all wisdom and spiritual understanding;*

10 That ye might walk worthy of the Lord unto all pleasing, being fruitful in every good work, and increasing in the knowledge of God;

11 Strengthened with all might, according to his glorious power, unto all patience and longsuffering with joyfulness;

12 Giving thanks unto the Father, which hath made us meet to be partakers of the inheritance of the saints in light:

13 Who hath delivered us from the power of darkness, and hath translated us into the kingdom of his dear Son:

14 In whom we have redemption through his blood, even the forgiveness of sins:

Romans 12:1 *I beseech you therefore, brethren, by the mercies of God, that ye present your bodies a living sacrifice, holy, acceptable unto God, which is your reasonable service.*

2 And be not conformed to this world: but be ye trans-

formed by the renewing of your mind, that ye may prove what is that good, and acceptable, and perfect, will of God.

James 1:22 *But be ye doers of the word, and not bearers only, deceiving your own selves.*

Psalm 119:33 *Teach me, O Lord, the way of thy statutes; and I shall keep it unto the end.*

34 Give me understanding and I shall keep thy law; yea, I shall observe it with my whole heart.

Scripture Discussion

The idea of "wisdom" and "spiritual understanding" seem to go hand in hand. When the multitudes requested that the apostles choose seven men reported to be honest and full of the Holy Spirit and wisdom (Acts 6:3), we see the coupling of these two words. The coupling of these words indicates that we need both wisdom and spiritual understanding if we are going to fulfill the will of God.

Paul says the Lord is working in the hearts and minds of many friends who are laboring for the Lord. Perhaps the knowledge of this should inspire us to pray as the apostle prays—that our friends might be helped and strengthened.

Pray that God's Servants Will Know the Will of God! The Apostle Paul says not to cease praying for God's servants because they need to be filled with the knowledge of God's will. They need wisdom and spiritual understanding.

In Romans 12:1, 2, the Apostle Paul writes that a life of service begins by knowing the will of God. A life of service begins with understanding the will of God. We would do well to pray that those whom we know—those who are in the service of the Lord, might be filled with the knowledge of God's will.

The word "filled" is a word which suggests being full.

It carries the idea of being filled to capacity, filled to overflowing. "The knowledge of his will" means knowing what the will of God is, understanding what the will of the Lord is. So therefore we need, first of all, as the Psalmist prayed in Psalm 119, to understand the will of God. God's will is reflected in the Word of God. Unless we know His Word, we will not know His will.

Pray that God's Servants Can "Walk Worthy"! Colossians 1:10 says that we need to "walk worthy of the Lord unto all pleasing." "Walking worthy" does not indicate that the Apostle Paul wanted us to know the will of God and the Word of God only for the sake of having a reservoir of truth in our minds. He wanted us to obey the Word of God.

"Worthy walking" leads to fruitfulness in our lives. Fruitfulness needs to be highlighted as we pray. Be fruitful in every good work and increase in the knowledge of God. We need to come more and more to understanding. We need to come more and more to knowing God! This knowledge of Him will result in our being strengthened with His power, strengthened with endurance and strengthened with the ability that comes from God.

In thinking about the Colossian Christians, the Apostle Paul reminded them of what God has done in their hearts and lives and what the Holy Spirit is still doing as they are presenting themselves for His service. In this passage, He has received a report from a friend called Epaphras, and he receives the report warmly. The report moves Paul to pray on behalf of the Colossian Christians.

Pray that God's Servants Can Move Forward with Thanksgiving! James 1:22 carries the same sentiment, when it indicates that we are to be doers of the Word and not hearers only. The idea of knowing the will of God that we might walk worthy of the Lord has to do with moving forward. Walking has to do with making progress. It has to do with development and with growing. These things follow one after the other.

Finally, prayer should involve a healthy amount of thanksgiving. The apostle says in Colossians 1:12 that we should give thanks to the Father who has made us qualified to be partakers of the inheritance of the saints in light.

May we continue to meditate on the wisdom that God has provided us about prayer!

Case Studies in Prayer

Instructions: The following exercises will lead you into an in-depth study of our Lord's prayer for Peter. Each of the four exercises consists of a series of "discovery" questions, followed by a summary question. The fifth exercise asks for a summary and an application. The sixth exercise asks you to apply the wisdom you gained from this "case study in prayer" to your private prayer life.

The Lord's Prayer for Peter

> And the Lord said, Simon, Simon, behold, Satan hath desired to have you that he may sift you as wheat: But I have prayed for thee that thy faith fail not: and when thou art converted, strengthen thy brethren. (Luke 22:31, 32)

1. Satan's Life Story

   Satan's peculiar history would cause him to take a special interest in a person like Peter.

   a. Ezekiel draws parallels between the life history of Satan and the life history of the King of Tyre.

Where did Satan originally reside? (Ezekiel 28:12-14)

b. What can be said of Satan's general intelligence? (Ezekiel 28:12)

c. How did Satan once dress? (Ezekiel 28:13)

d. What changed Satan's general state of affairs? (Ezekiel 28:17-19; Luke 10:18; Revelation 12:7-8)

e. What will Satan's future be? (Ezekiel 28:18-19; Isaiah 14:12-17; Revelation 12:10-11; 20:2; 20:3, 7, 8-10)

f. Summary Question: The Lord must have realized Peter had certain weaknesses that Satan would try to manipulate. (Luke 22:23-31) Considering the general history and future of Satan, why would our Lord say that He would be interested in Peter?

2. Satan as the Head of an Evil World System

Satan occupies a particular place of prominence in today's evil world system.

a. What is one of the things that Satan has always wanted to hinder? (Zechariah 3:1)

b. Of what is Satan the head? (Matthew 9:34; 12:26; 8:29)

c. How can Satan's evil system affect the churches that are not on one accord? (Revelation 2:9-13; Matthew 13:18-23; 8:20, 31-33, 39-44)

d. What freedoms and limitations does God place on Satan in the world? (Job 1:6—2:6; 1 John 2:1)

e. Summary Question: Describe Satan's position in the world. Given his position, how might he try to destroy Peter? What references does our Lord make to this when He tells Peter that He is praying for him?

3. Satan's Objectives

Jesus knew what Satan's goals were.

a. What had been one of Satan's primary objectives? (John 13:27; 6:70; Luke 22:53)
b. What is another of Satan's chief objectives? (John 8:44)
c. What is another of Satan's objectives? (Matthew 13:19-39)
d. What else had been one of Satan's primary objectives? (Revelation 20:10)
e. What is yet another of Satan's objectives? (Job 1:6-11; 1 Corinthians 5:1-5; 1 Timothy 1:20)
f. Summary Question: Consider your answers to questions a-e. Then summarize some of the goals and objectives of Satan. Considering these, shed some more light on what Jesus meant when He said that Satan had a special interest in Peter.

4. Peter's Weaknesses

Jesus knew Peter's weaknesses.

a. What was one of Peter's weaknesses of which Satan might take advantage? (Matthew 16:21-23; Mark 8:31-33)
b. What is another of Peter's weaknesses in which Satan might be interested? (Matthew 17:1-5; Mark 9:2-7; Luke 9:28-35)
c. What is one of Peter's traits of which Satan might take advantage? (Matthew 26:37-41; Mark 14:32-38)
d. What is yet another of Peter's traits that might interest Satan? (Matthew 26:51-52; John 18:10-11)
e. During the events leading up to Christ's crucifixion, what types of traits did Peter display in which Satan was certainly interested? (Mark

14:66-72; Luke 22:55-62; John 18:15-18, 25-27)

f. What was yet another trait that Satan might exploit? (Luke 24:1-12; John 20:1-10)

g. Summary Question: Review your answers to questions a-f. Then summarize Peter's general personality traits. In light of these traits, present some of the reasons Jesus may have thought that Satan desired to have Peter.

5. Summary Exercise: Considering Satan's history, his network of evil, his general goals and objectives and Peter's weaknesses, review Peter's role in the formation of the early church (Acts 1, 2). In light of Peter's future role, present reasons why Jesus might have seen fit to pray for Peter, in particular.

6. Application: Review some of Peter's personality traits again. Then take a look inside. Have you ever exhibited any of these tendencies? Does Peter remind you of any other of God's servants? If so, make it a high priority for you to pray for the protection of yourself and for the protection of each of God's servants from Satan's powerful forces of evil that would desire to "sift" us all as wheat.

CHAPTER ELEVEN

Praying for World Evangelism

Many missonaries send their requests for prayer through magazines and newspaper articles.

from Scripture
Isaiah 52:7 *How beautiful upon the mountains are the
feet of him that bringeth good tidings, that publisheth
peace; that bringeth good tidings of good, that publisheth
salvation; that saith unto Zion, Thy God reigneth!*
*8 Thy watchmen shall lift up the voice; with the voice
together shall they sing; for they shall see eye to eye, when
the Lord shall bring again Zion.*
*9 Break forth into joy, sing together, ye waste places
of Jerusalem: for the Lord hath comforted his people, he
hath redeemed Jerusalem.*
*10 The Lord hath made bare his holy arm in the eyes
of all the nations; and all the ends of the earth shall see
the salvation of our God.*
*11 Depart ye, depart ye, go ye out from thence, touch
no unclean thing; go ye out of the midst of her, be ye
clean, that bear the vessels of the Lord.*
*12 For ye shall not go out with haste, nor go by flight:
for the Lord will go before you; and the God of Israel will
be your reward.*
*13 Behold, my servant shall deal prudently, he shall
be exalted and extolled, and be very high.*
*14 As many were astonished at thee; his visage was
so marred more than any man, and his form more than
the sons of men:*
*15 So shall he sprinkle many nations; the kings shall
shut their mouths at him: for that which had not been*

told them shall they see; and that which they had not heard shall they consider.

Matthew 28:18 *All power is given unto me in heaven and in earth.*

19 Go ye therefore, and teach all nations, baptizing them in the name of the Father, and of the Son, and of the Holy Ghost:

20 Teaching them to observe all things whatsoever I have commanded you: and, lo, I am with you always, even unto the end of the world. Amen.

Scripture Discussion

Billy Graham, Bishop Desmond Tutu, and Dr. George Sweeting are among God's many servants who carry the Gospel to various countries of the world. I was reminded of this as I thumbed through *Moody Monthly* and saw two very practical ways in which prayer might help them and us in our daily evangelistic efforts.

We should be inclined to pray as we flip through magazines and articles. So many prayer requests are circulated in this way. This is one way in which prayer becomes very practical. Another way prayer requests come to us is through the mail.

In one article, called "Talking it Over," Dr. Sweeting mentioned six prayer requests he received as he engaged in evangelistic work in Korea, preaching to an audience of Korean pastors. While the occasion for these particular prayer requests has passed, the principles illustrated remain.

The occasion for Dr. Sweeting being in Korea was the 100th anniversary of missions in Korea, and that certainly is a testimony to the fact that God has kept alive and opened the doors there. After so many years, there are a great number of Koreans who are being sent out as missionaries to other places.

Pray for a Hunger for God. First of all, Dr. Sweeting asked for prayer for Korea itself. He asked that we pray for a hunger and thirst among the people for God and for His Word—particularly among Korean brothers and sisters in Christ.

His request reminded me of, when as a youngster, some of the earliest missionaries that I heard speak were two ladies from Korea. They had brought a Korean young girl along with them.

Seeing a live missionary and hearing their report was probably one of the most interesting things that I have ever heard. When it comes to their missionary outreach, Korean brothers and sisters have always had a place in my affection.

Pray for the Preachers of the Word. Sweeting also asked that we pray that he will be aware of spiritual needs and that people will be convicted of sin. As we think of men of God who preach the Word in various places, we don't often realize the need they have to have the Holy Spirit prepare the hearts of those who will be listening to their sermons. However, it is very vital and valid for him to request that we pray to this end.

Pray for Missionary Outreach. Sweeting's third request was that the Korean Evangelical Church increase its contributions to World Mission Outreach. Sweeting said that presently more than 280 Korean missionaries serve in other lands. That is an encouraging sign of expansion. This is certainly something for which we need to rejoice and for which we can praise God!

Pray for Protection from Materialism. Sweeting's fourth request was that we pray that Korean Christian Evangelicals will not become dulled by a growing problem of materialism. Materialism is a growing problem for all of us. Lifestyles today provide us with so many of the things that are desirable to the flesh. Often we're given over, unconsciously, to materialism; therefore, we need to pray that, in the midst of the zeal and desire to carry forth the Word of God, that this zeal might not be dulled by the growing problem of materialism.

Pray for Youth in Other Countries. Sweeting's fifth request was that we pray for God's continued blessing among the college population of Korea. There are 100 colleges and universities there, and many of the young people have made a profession of faith in Christ. This is certainly something for which to praise God.

We need to pray that their growth in Christ might continue. The Apostle Paul, as he wrote to the Colossian Christians said that he'd heard of their faith in the Lord Jesus and he ceased not to pray for them. That needs to be our position as well.

Pray for Christian Broadcasting. Sweeting's sixth request was that we pray for the success of Korean radio, particularly the missionary station which reaches Korea, parts of China and Russia.

Billy Graham, in his Amsterdam ministry, also made a series of requests for prayer. At the time of his requests, he was going to be a part of a conference of itinerant evangelists. The team would consist of men from various parts of the world. Some of these men are not well known, but they are very definitely men who have a need for our prayers.

Billy Graham presented the following list of prayer requests in relationship to his work in Amsterdam.

Pray for the Physical Strength of God's Workers. Billy Graham asked that we pray for the physical strength of his staff. The team had a tremendous work load. Their work included assembling the program and designing various activities. To accomplish all of this, it was vitally necessary that they have physical strength. Many of the staff members traveled from great distances and they needed journeying mercies as they came to the conference.

Pray for the Conference Participants. Prayer was needed, not only for the members of the staff, but for those who attended the conference. They, too, came from great distances. Their hearts were hungry for different kinds of needs. They all had questions that were germaine to their particular local regions.

Prayer was needed that their needs would be met through the conference main sessions and workshops. Prayer was needed that all conference speakers would be used by the Holy Spirit to communicate God's purpose in these meetings. Many conferences have a great number of speakers, and each one of them seeks to be uniquely used of the Lord in meeting the needs of individuals that are sitting before them.

Sometimes in the rush and hustle of the preparation, when we present a conference, we are not aware or are constantly cognizant of the fact that the Holy Spirit must be in charge every moment and in all that is said. We need to pray for the speakers that they might communicate the Word as the Holy Spirit would have them do it.

Also, in connection with this, Billy Graham asked that we pray for the financial needs of conference participants as well. Most third world participants have needed financial subsidies.

Pray for Spiritual Revival. Billy Graham asked that we pray for the beginning of genuine spiritual revival in many parts of the world. Every year, people go to conferences and evangelistic crusades such as Billy Graham's for spiritual revival. They come from great distances, from a variety of backgrounds and from many different countries. It is important that we pray that such people first be united and that their enthusiasm would be sustained when they go back to their local places of residence. Then we should pray that their personal ministries might benefit greatly from what has been done at such conferences.

To that end, Bishop Desmond Tutu faces tremendous odds and obstacles as he seeks to communicate hope to the Black people of South Africa, and at the same time challenge the government of that country to stop the oppression. Pray for this man and other African Christians who are under constant pressure.

May we continue to pray for God's work in Korea, God's work in Amsterdam, God's work in South Africa, and God's work throughout the world. Let us pray that God will grant our requests in a way that only He can, and in a way that is according to His will.

Case Studies in Prayer

Instructions: The following exercises will lead you into an in-depth study of the role of prayer in the Apostle Paul's outreach to the New Testament Church at Rome. Each of the first four exercises consists of a series of "discovery" questions, followed by a summary question. The fifth exercise asks for a summary and an application.

The sixth exercise asks you to apply the wisdom you gained from this "case study in prayer" to your private prayer life.

Prayer for the Church at Rome

> First, I thank my God through Jesus Christ for you all, that your faith is spoken of throughout the whole world. For God is my witness, whom I serve with my spirit in the gospel of his Son, that without ceasing I make mention of you always in my prayers;
>
> Making request, if by any means now at

by the will of God to come unto you. For I long to see you, that I may impart unto you some spiritual gift, to the end ye may be established; That is, that I may be comforted together with you by the mutual faith both of you and me.

Now I would not have you ignorant, brethren, that oftentimes I purposed to come unto you, (but was let hitherto,) that I might have some fruit among you also, even as among other Gentiles. I am debtor both to the Greeks, and to the Barbarians; both to the wise, and to the unwise. So, as much as in me is, I am ready to preach the gospel to you that are at Rome also. (Romans 1:8-15)

1. The Church at Rome

The Apostle Paul was interested in both the spiritual and practical needs of the members of the church at Rome.

a. What evidence is there that the church at Rome was more than a casual interest of the Apostle Paul? (Acts 19:21; Romans 1:1, 7-16; 15:20-24)

b. Describe the person who delivered the Epistle of Romans to the church at Rome. (Romans 16:1-2)

c. The Apostle Paul tells the members of the Roman Church that, on a particular occasion, he appears to have given social action a higher priority than preaching to them. Explain the circumstances surrounding this. (Romans 15:24-29; 1 Corinthians 16:1-4; 2 Corinthians 8, 9).

d. How might Christianity have gotten into Rome initially? (Acts 2:1-5, 10)

e. Summary Question: Considering Romans 1:8-15

and what you examined in questions a-d, compose a hypothetical section of the Apostle Paul's prayer list concerning the church at Rome. The list should contain both practical and spiritual concerns.

2. Prayer for Priscilla and Aquilla

The Apostle Paul's prayer list must have contained specific requests for Priscilla and Aquilla—members of the church at Rome.

a. Who were Priscilla and Aquilla? (Acts 18:1-2, 18; Romans 16:3-4)

b. Where was Aquilla born? (Acts 18:2)

c. Where did the Apostle Paul originally meet Aquilla? (Acts 18:1)

d. How did Aquilla happen to come to Corinth? (Acts 18:2)

e. What did the Apostle Paul and Aquilla have in common? (Acts 18:3)

f. With whom did Priscilla and Aquilla travel? (Acts 18:18)

g. What role did Priscilla and Aquilla play in the spreading of Christianity? (Acts 18:24-26; 1 Corinthians 16:19; Romans 16:3-5)

h. What evidence is there that Priscilla's role extended beyond the kitchen? (Acts 18:26)

i. Summary Question: Dr. Banks recommended that we pray for people and their ministries, based on our sense of what they might need and based on their specific requests. If the Apostle Paul had a prayer list containing the needs of Priscilla and Aquilla, what types of things might it have contained?

3. Prayers for the Saints

There were a number of other people in the church at Rome for whom the Apostle Paul prayed.

a. Who was one of the early converts of the Apostle Paul who belonged to the church at Rome? (Romans 16:5)

b. Name six laborers who were in the church at Rome. (16:6, 9, 10, 12)

c. Name two people whom Paul called "beloved." (16:8, 9)

d. Name two people who had been fellow prisoners with Paul, but who now belonged to the church at Rome. (16:7)

e. Name five households (or families) that are mentioned among the churches at Rome. (16:10-11, 13-15)

f. Was the church at Rome in perfect harmony? Explain. (16:17-18)

g. Summary Question: If you were to develop a section of the Apostle Paul's prayer list, containing requests for these members of the church at Rome, what types of needs might the prayer list contain?

4. The Apostle Paul's Staff

The Apostle Paul also needed prayer for his ministry—particularly for those who labored with him in his missionary outreach.

a. What role did Timothy play in the Apostle Paul's ministry? (Acts 16:1-5; 17:13-15; Philippians 2:19-20, 22-23; 1 Thessalonians 1:1-2; 3:1-2;

2 Thessalonians 1:1-3; Romans 16:21)

b. What are some of the specific responsibilities that Timothy had? (2 Timothy 1:1-8; 1 Timothy 3:11-15; 4:6, 12-14; 5:1, 3-10, 19-20; 1 Timothy 3:1-13)

c. What role did Lucius play in the church? (Romans 16:21; Acts 13:1)

d. What is known about Jason? (Romans 16:21; Acts 17:5-9)

e. Who is the likely identity of Sosipater? (Romans 16:21; Acts 20:4)

f. What is known about Tertius? (Romans 16:22)

g. What is known about Gaius? (Romans 16:23; 1 Corinthians 1:14)

h. What is known about Erastus? (Acts 19:22; Romans 16:23; 2 Timothy 4:20)

i. What is known of Quartus? (Romans 16:23)

j. Summary Question: If you had been a Christian at Rome, and you were praying for the Apostle Paul and his staff, you might have developed a prayer list of concerns for them. Consider your answers to a-i above. What types of needs might that prayer list contain?

5. Summary Exercise: Dr. Banks said that, when we pray for God's work throughout the world, that we should pray for: a) the spread of the Gospel, b) the preaching of the Word, c) the missionary outreach, d) protection from materialism, e) redemption of world youth, f) Christian media, g) physical strength of God's workers, h) spiritual revival, i) salvation of souls.

   In what ways do Paul's prayers (cited above in Romans 1) for the Roman Church reflect these areas of concern?

6. Application: Develop a list of Christians (such as Bishop Desmond Tutu and others) who are working to spread the Gospel in other countries. Then develop a prayer list of needs for them. As you develop the list, consider Dr. Banks' list of possible concern areas.

CHAPTER TWELVE

Christ's Body Praying

Prayer is to be practiced in solitude, private and public. Attention should be given to private prayer, to public prayer and to professional prayer.

from Scripture

1 Kings 8:1 *Then Solomon assembled the elders of*
Israel, and all the heads of the tribes, the chief of the
fathers of the children of Israel, unto king Solomon in
Jerusalem, that they might bring up the ark of the cove-
nant of the Lord out of the city of David, which is Zion.
2 And all the men of Israel assembled themselves
unto king Solomon at the feast in the month Ethanim,
which is the seventh month.
22 And Solomon stood before the altar of the Lord in
the presence of all the congregation of Israel, and spread
forth his hands toward heaven:
23 And he said, Lord God of Israel, there is no God
like thee, in heaven above, or on earth beneath, who
keepest covenant and mercy with thy servants that walk
before thee with all their heart:
24 Who hast kept with thy servant David my father
that thou promisedst him: thou spakest also with thy
mouth, and hast fulfilled it with thine hand, as it is this
day.
25 Therefore now, Lord God of Israel, keep with thy
servant David my father that thou promisedst him, say-
ing, There shall not fail thee a man in my sight to sit on
the throne of Israel; so that thy children take heed to
their way, that they walk before me as thou hast walked

before me.
26 *And now, O God of Israel, let thy word, I pray*
thee, be verified, which thou spakest unto thy servant
David my father.
27 *But will God indeed dwell on the earth? behold,*
the heaven and heaven of heavens cannot contain thee;
how much less this house that I have builded?
28 *Yet have thou respect unto the prayer of thy ser-*
vant, and to his supplication, O Lord my God, to hearken
unto the cry and to the prayer, which thy servant prayeth
before thee today:
29 *That thine eyes may be open toward this house*
night and day, even toward the place of which thou hast
said, My name shall be there: that thou mayest hearken
unto the prayer which thy servant shall make toward
this place.
30 *And hearken thou to the supplication of thy ser-*
vant, and of thy people Israel, when they shall pray
toward this place: and hear thou in heaven thy dwelling-
place: and when thou hearest, forgive.

Scripture Discussion

The *International Standard Bible Encyclopedia* includes five summary statements concerning prayer. It says:

> Prayer is the highest exercise of man's spiritual nature. It is natural to the soul; even in perfect accord with God. It is not only the expression of need; the supply of which is sought of God; by the example of Christ, it is the highest expression of trust, submission and union with God.
>
> It is practical, both in solitude or private and in society or public...It is both public and intercessory. It may be accompanied

> by the plea of Christ's name, and for Christ's sake. It should be based upon the merit and intercession of Christ, and should be addressed to God in accordance with His will. Its purpose is the good of the one who is praying and for God's kingdom. [1]

This summary statement takes into account much of what can be said concerning prayer. It points out that prayer is to be practiced in solitude, private and public. Attention should be given to private prayer, to public prayer and to professional prayer.

Private Prayer. Private prayer, of course, is done in the quietness of one's "closet." It is that expression of the heart and soul which is concerned with those who are near. The Lord Jesus Christ recommended that when we pray we should enter our closet. Then we should shut the door. We can pray to our Father in secret. The words "secret" and "private" are interchangeable in this matter of prayer.

Private prayer can be spontaneous. We have many, many examples of this. It is the kind of prayer that comes directly from the heart, unrehearsed. An example is Peter's prayer as he was on the water, walking toward the Lord Jesus Christ and about to sink. He said, "Lord, save me, I perish." That was spontaneous. It came directly from a need and from Peter's heart.

When we think of private prayer, we think of what the Lord Jesus Christ said in Matthew the sixth chapter. There, He exhorted those who asked Him what prayer was. He told them that they should enter into their secret closet and pray.

We realize that there are many instances and many places in the Word of God where we can find this same kind of exhortation concerning private prayer. The one that strikes us with great force is in Psalms chapter 6. In verse 6, the psalmist shares some of his experiences.

He says:

> I am weary with my groaning; all the night make I my bed to swim; I water my couch with my tears. Mine eye is consumed because of grief; it waxeth old because of all mine enemies...Let all mine enemies be ashamed and sore vexed: let them return and be ashamed suddenly. (Psalm 6:6-7, 10)

This is a private prayer. The psalmist, here, is struggling with some inner conflict or is reacting to some persecution—something that has come upon him from without. Private prayer then, is that which is done as we pour out our soul to God in a secret place—in a private place, in our "closet," where sometimes we can be freer. The flow of our innermost thoughts can be uninhibited while we are in private prayer. Private prayer is very vital and necessary.

Public Prayer. Then there is public prayer. This type of prayer takes place in groups, usually at public occasions and worship services.

The Apostle Paul said to Timothy as he wrote to him concerning the matter of his conduct in the ministry, that Timothy should give attention to the public reading of the Scriptures. He also suggested that prayer remain in the congregation. The element of public prayer is very vital and very necessary.

Perhaps one of the simplest and earliest of the examples of corporate or public prayer is in Acts the first chapter. In this chapter, our Lord Jesus Christ has already separated from His disciples (1:10, 11). The disciples had beheld Him as He went out of their sight and as a cloud had received Him. At that time, He had given them a charge to return to Jerusalem. They had returned to Jerusalem near the Mount of Olives and to the upper room. There they continued for ten days, praying until the day of Pentecost was fully come (2:1).

With them were Peter, James, John, Andrew, Philip, Thomas, Bartholomew, Matthew, James, Simon Zealot, Judas the brother of James, Mary the mother of Jesus, other women and the brothers of Jesus.

We are not given the names of all of those who were there. However, the Scripture says that there were about 120 in number. These people prayed together in corporate or public prayer. They all continued in prayer with one accord.

Prior to this, there had been no time when our Lord Jesus gathered with His disciples and said, "Let's have a prayer meeting." A prayer meeting was something that was foreign to the disciples. However, now they learned that public prayer was necessary for mutual strengthening—for a sense of oneness among believers.

Together, we come boldly to the throne of grace that we may obtain mercy and find grace to help in the time of need (Hebrews 4:16). We should have both private and public or corporate prayer. One does not exclude the other. If we pray privately, that does not mean that we do not pray publicly. If we pray publicly, that does not mean that we do not pray privately.

Professional Prayer. Professional prayer takes place at very special occasions, inaugurations, national events or civic occasions. The prayer of Solomon (1 Kings 8) when he dedicated the temple is an example of public prayer.

The term "professional" does not suggest that we are putting a type of "studied air" around this type of prayer. One does not need to go and learn a technique or a particular phraseology to pray in this way. That is not the idea. What makes prayer professional can be learned from a study of Solomon's prayer in the dedication of the temple.

The prayer is quite lengthy. It is not quoted in its entirety here. The temple which Solomon was dedicating represented a very important segment in the life of the people of Israel. When the tabernacle had originally been erected, there was no mention of praying as such. However, when it was completed, the glory of God filled it. As the glory of God filled the tabernacle (Exodus 40), the priests were not ministering. Those leaders in prayer were not exercising their responsibilities.

However, God owned this house. God said, "This is the place of my presence." The people were in awe before Him. At the time of Solomon's prayer, the temple had been erected. The temple contained remnants of the original tabernacle—the things that were used earlier as Moses was led of God to construct the tabernacle in the wilderness.

There are very beautiful elements in Solomon's prayer. First of all, there is the honor of God. There is the blessing of God on this house. This house is a very special and unique place. The Lord Jesus Christ referred to it as a house of prayer when He came and chased away the money changers (John 2). Solomon, in dedicating the house, recognized that it was God's house and it was a place of God's presence.

Professional prayer is very important—just as is private and public or corporate prayer.

Preparing for All Kinds of Prayer with Faith. There should be preparation for all types of prayer. To pray effectively and to communicate one's need to God, we must prepare. This means that "he that cometh to God must believe that he is, and that he is a rewarder of them that diligently seek him" (Hebrews 11:6). We need to keep this particular fact uppermost in our minds.

When we come to God, we must believe that He exists. Certainly prayer is in one sense a coming to God. It is a relating oneself to Him. It is a communion with God. And so one who comes to Him must believe that God exists. Those who seek God in this way are rewarded.

"Faith is the substance of things hoped for, the evidence of things not seen" (Hebrews 11:1). The things hoped for are those things in our souls where there is hope.

Contemplating Our Needs. There are four considerations when we pray—regardless of the form of prayer. First of all, we should study our own heart's needs. We should contemplate our needs. Then we should evaluate ourselves in the light of what we have come to understand from the word of God.

To be in right relations with Him and to have a life of obedience, we must practice piety. If we do not analyze ourselves, if we do not periodically come to a study of our own needs, we will not be prepared for prayer.

God has made rich resources available to us. Every resource we need has been made available to us by Him. As we read the Word of God, we can read it with pencil in hand and as we read from one portion and are blessed through the lives of individuals, through the statements, through what God has said, we can be sensitive to a need that we have. Then we can pray in that regard.

We need to open our heart to God as we read His Word. We need to read with the idea in mind that we're coming to a Book that was given to us. It is a Word. It is a record that was given to us by the almighty God, our Creator. It was given to us by the one who has revealed Himself to us in this Book. We should become increasingly more knowledgeable of Him.

We must therefore give attention to what He has said concerning Himself in His Word. We need to be very studious about this. Take a note pad, file cards, or whatever, to keep a record in a separate book. Read with the Word open, with a view to hearing what God is saying. You will certainly be exposed at that particular point of what your heart needs as you heed God's Word.

The psalmist said that "the entrance of thy words giveth light" (Psalm 119:130). The word "light" has to do with knowledge and understanding. As we read the

Word, we need that understanding. We need that light. We need to keep in mind that reading the Word is also preparing for prayer.

Recognizing Our Strengths and Weaknesses. We need to recognize our strengths and weaknesses in carrying out the ministry which God has given us. We've come to know what weaknesses we have as we compare ourselves with people in the Word of God. We become aware of our weaknesses. Then we know what our needs are.

Dr. Roy Loren, in a book written years ago entitled, *Meet Yourself in the Bible,* says that there are characters in the Bible with whom we can identify. As we read about the particular character with whom we identify, the experiences of that individual remind us of the struggles in which we are involved. These characters also show us how to overcome our weaknesses. We can also identify strengths in the lives of these characters. Finding our strength is a wonderful thing to do. It can help us to supplant our weaknesses.

Making a Prayer List. We should make a prayer list for intercession. This applies to all forms of prayer. Many, many times during the day we encounter different individuals as we read magazines. We should list these persons. We ought to list their requests for prayer. This is part of preparing for prayer. God has made many rich promises to us. He has told us under certain circumstances that He will not hear. He has told us in other situations that He will hear. His ear is opened.

His heart is attuned to us and our needs. We need therefore to study and prepare our hearts and minds for prayer. I believe preparing for prayer is engaging in worship service. We realize that worship is a vital necessity in our lives. Together with prayer, it is a very high priority for our spiritual life. Just as we sometimes don't prepare for worship, we frequently don't prepare for prayer. However, preparation is a vital necessity.

We need to keep that in mind.

May God mightily use this chapter to stimulate our prayer life.

1. James Orr (Editor), *International Standard Bible Encyclopedia* (Chicago: Howard-Severance, 1915), Volume IV, pp. 2430-33.

Case Studies in Prayer

Instructions: The following exercises will lead you into an in-depth study of the corporate or public prayer of the people of Nineveh during the time of Jonah. Each of the first four exercises consists of a series of "discovery" questions, followed by a summary question. The fifth exercise asks for a summary and an application.

The sixth exercise asks you to apply the wisdom you gained from this "case study in prayer" to your private prayer life.

The Prayer of the People of Nineveh

> So the people of Nineveh believed God, and proclaimed a fast, and put on sackcloth, from the greatest of them even to the least of them. For word came unto the king of Nineveh, and he arose from his throne, and he laid his robe from Him, and covered him with sackcloth, and sat in ashes.
>
> And he caused it to be proclaimed and published through Nineveh by the decree of the king and his nobles, saying, Let neither man nor beast, herd nor flock, taste anything: let them not feed, nor drink water: But let man and beast be covered with sackcloth, and cry mightily unto God: yea,

let them turn every one from his evil way, and from the violence that is in their hands.

Who can tell if God will turn and repent, and turn away from his fierce anger, that we perish not? And God saw their works, that they turned from their evil way; and God repented of the evil, that he had said that he would do unto them; and he did it not. (Jonah 3:5-10)

1. Nineveh

Nineveh's history as a people is reflected in their prayer to God.

a. Who was the founder of Nineveh? (Genesis 10:8-10)

b. What is the likely race of Nimrod? (Genesis 10:1, 6, 8-9)

c. What type of city was Nineveh? (Jonah 3:3)

d. What were some of the problems Nineveh had? (Nahum 2:1—3:19; Zephaniah 2:13-15; Jonah 1:2; 3:3-4)

e. Who was sent to minister to Nineveh? (Jonah 1:1-2)

f. What was Jonah to tell Nineveh? (Jonah 1:2; 3:2)

g. How did Nineveh respond to Jonah's preaching? (3:5)

h. Summary Question: Provide an overview of the history of Nineveh and how that history is reflected in the prayer of Nineveh. (3:6-10)

2. Fasting

By fasting, the people of Nineveh were sending a very special message to God.

a. What was one reason for fasting in Hebrew

culture? (1 Samuel 7:6; 1 Kings 1:20-29; Nehemiah 1:3-9; Numbers 29:7)

b. What were some reasons for fasting publicly as a group? (Leviticus 23:26-29; 2 Chronicles 20:1-4; Ezra 8:21; Esther 4:15-17; 1 Samuel 7:6)

c. What were the conditions of a fast? (Leviticus 23:27-29)

d. What was another meaning of fasting? (1 Samuel 1:7; 20:34; 31:11-13; 2 Samuel 1:12; Ezra 10:6; Judges 20:25-26)

e. What was another meaning of fasting? (2 Samuel 12:15-16; Luke 2:36-38)

f. What was another meaning of fasting? (2 Chronicles 20:3; Joel 1:14-15)

g. In what ways could fasting be abused? (Matthew 6:16; 1 Kings 21:1-10; Isaiah 58:3-9; Jeremiah 14:10-12)

h. What is a good use for private fasting? (Matthew 17:20-21; Mark 9:28-29; Acts 16:23)

i. Summary Question: Using your answers to questions a-h as a guide, explain what the people of Nineveh were saying to God when they fasted.

3. Sackcloth

When the people of Nineveh put on sackcloth, they were sending a very special message forth to God.

a. What did sackcloth look like? (Revelation 6:12; Isaiah 50:3)

b. In Jewish culture, for what was sackcloth generally used? (Genesis 37:34; 42:25; Joshua 9:4; Esther 4:1-4)

c. Where, on the body, was sackcloth worn? (2 Kings 6:30; Job 16:15; Isaiah 32:11; Jonah 3:6)

d. What did girding in sackcloth symbolize? (Psalm 35:13; 69:9-13; Isaiah 3:18-26; 15:1-4; 22:10-14; 32:9-15)

e. What did putting off of sackcloth symbolize? (Psalm 30:11-12)

f. Summary Question: Considering your answers to questions a-e, when the people of Nineveh put on sackcloth, what were they saying to God?

4. Ashes

When the king of Nineveh sat in ashes, he was sending a very special message to God.

a. When Job once sat among the ashes, what was he expressing to God? (Job 2:7-8; 42:1-6)

b. If the "children of Benjamin" were to heed Jeremiah's warning and "wallow themselves in ashes," what should they, collectively, have said to God? (Jeremiah 6:26)

c. What had sackcloth and ashes come to mean in the Jewish culture? (Matthew 11:21)

d. Summary Question: Considering your answers to questions a-c, when the king of Nineveh sat in ashes, what was he saying to God? (Jonah 3:6)

5. Summary Exercise: Using the information gathered in questions 1-4, compose a hypothetical prayer which expresses what the people of Nineveh were saying to God when they put on sackcloth, sat in ashes and fasted.

6. Application: The prayer of the people of Nineveh is what Dr. Banks would classify as a public or corporate prayer. Like other prayers, Dr. Banks says that it should reflect: a) faith, b) an expression

of our needs, c) an acknowledgment of our strengths and weaknesses, and d) intercession for others.

Are there ways in which your church, as a body of believers, could follow the example of the people of Nineveh and engage in corporate (or public) prayers that follow Dr. Banks' guidelines? Are there ways that these prayers could be expressed in a way that sends forth some of the messages that the people of Nineveh sent forth to God?

Bibliography

Adeney, Carol. *This Morning with God.* Downer's Grove: Inter-Varsity Press, 1978.

Alexander, John W. *Morning Watch.* Downer's Grove: Inter-Varsity Press, 1980.

Becker, Nancy. "Teaching People to Pray." *Leadership,* Volume 5, No. 1, 106-108 Winter, 1984.

Bewes, Richard. *Talking about Prayer.* Downer's Grove: Inter-Varsity Press, 1980.

Blackwood, Andrew J. *Prayers For All Occasions.* Grand Rapids: Baker Book House, 1960.

Burgess, F. J. and D. B. Proudlove. *Watching unto Prayer.* London: Butterworth Press, 1944.

Carter, Harold A. *The Prayer Tradition of Black People.* Baltimore: Gateway Press, 1985.

Chadwick, Samuel. *The Path of Prayer.* London: Hodder and Stoughton, 1931.

Chappell, Clovis. *Seven Words.* Grand Rapids: Baker Book House, 1976.

Clark, Kelly James. *Quiet Times for Christian Growth.* Downer's Grove: Inter-Varsity Press, 1976.

Foster, Richard J. *Meditative Prayer.* Downer's Grove: Inter-Varsity Press, 1986.

Goodrich, C. A. *Bible History of Prayer.* London: Case, Tiffany, Hartford, 1850.

Gordon, S. D. *A Miscellany of Quiet Talks.* London: Pickering and Inglish, 1940.

Griffiths, Michael. *The Example of Jesus.* Downer's Grove: Inter-Varsity Press, 1985.

Hubbard, David Allen. *The Practice of Prayer.* Downer's Grove: Inter-Varsity Press, 1983.

Hummell, Charles. *Filled with the Spirit.* Downer's Grove: Inter-Varsity Press, 1981.

Hunter, W. Bingham. *The God Who Hears.* Downer's Grove: Inter-Varsity Press, 1986.

Inter-Varsity Christian Fellowship. *First Mornings with God.* Downer's Grove: Inter-Varsity Press, 1986.

———. *Grow Your Christian Life.* Downer's Grove: Inter-Varsity Press, 1972.

———. *The Quiet Time.* Downer's Grove: Inter-Varsity Press, 1980.

King, Guy H. *Prayer Secrets.* London: Marshall, Morgan and Scott, 1940.

Kunz, Marilyn. *Patterns for Living with God.* Downer's Grove: Inter-Varsity Press, 1961.

LePeau, Phyllis and Andrew. *Faith That Works.* Downer's Grove: Inter-Varsity Press, 1987.

Lockyer, Herbert, Litt. D. *All the Prayers of the Bible.* Grand Rapids: Zondervan Publishing House, 1959.

Lofton, Fred C. *Teach Us to Pray.* Elgin: Progressive Baptist Publishing House, 1980.

McFadyen, J. E. *The Prayers of the Bible.* London: Hodder and Stoughton, 1906.

Mcintyre, David M. *The Prayer Life of Our Lord.* Marshall, Morgan and Scott, 1920.

McLeish, James. *Faithful Witness.* Downer's Grove: Inter-Varsity Press, 1985.

Munger, Robert. *My Heart Christ's Home.* Downer's Grove: Inter-Varsity Press, 1986.

Packer, James I. *Knowing God.* Downer's Grove: Inter-Varsity Press, 1975.

Patterson, John. *How to Pray Together.* Downer's

Grove: Inter-Varsity Press, 1951.

Peterson, Eugene. *Earth & Altar.* Downer's Grove: Inter-Varsity Press, 1985.

Pink, A. W. *The Beatitudes and The Lord's Prayer.* Grand Rapids: Baker Book House, 1979.

Price, Frederick. *How Faith Works.* Tulsa: Harrison House, 1976.

———. *How to Obtain Strong Faith* - Six Principles. Tulsa: Harrison House, 1980.

———. *Foolishness, or Presumption.* Tulsa: Harrison House, 1983.

———. *Now Faith Is.* Tulsa: Harrison House, 1983.

Scruggs, Julius Richard. *God is Faithful.* Valley Forge: Judson Press, 1985.

Simcox, Carroll. *Prayer—The Divine Dialogue.* Downer's Grove: Inter-Varsity Press, 1985.

Smith, Blaine. *Knowing God's Will.* Downer's Grove: Inter-Varsity Press, 1979.

Stott, John. *Being a Christian.* Downer's Grove: Inter-Varsity Press, 1957.

Thomas, Latta. *Biblical Faith and the Black American.* Valley Forge: Judson Press, 1976.

Torrey, R. A. *Teach Us to Pray.* Chicago: Moody Press, 1982.

———. *The Power of Prayer and the Prayer of Power.* Grand Rapids: Zondervan Publishing House, 1955.

Trobisch, Walter. *Martin Luther's Quiet Time.* Downer's Grove: Inter-Varsity Press, 1975.

Trull, Joe E. *The Seven Last Words of the Risen Christ.* Grand Rapids: Baker Book House, 1985.

Vaughan, C. J. *The Prayers of Jesus Christ.* London: Macmillan and Co., 1891.

White, John. *Daring to Draw Near.* Grand Rapids:

Inter-Varsity Press, 1977.
———. *The Fight.* Grand Rapids: Inter-Varsity Press, 1976.